SINGLE WORLD, DIVIDED NATIONS?

ROBERT Z. LAWRENCE

SINGLE WORLD, DIVIDED NATIONS?

International Trade and OECD Labor Markets

BROOKINGS INSTITUTION PRESS

OECD DEVELOPMENT CENTRE

Copyright © 1996
ORGANISATION FOR ECONOMIC CO-OPERATION AND DEVELOPMENT
2 rue André-Pascal, 75775 Paris Cedex 16, France

Library of Congress Cataloging-in-Publication data

Lawrence, Robert Z., 1949–
    Single world, divided nations? : international trade and OECD
labor markets / by Robert Z. Lawrence
    p. cm.
    Includes bibliographical references and index.
    ISBN 0-8157-5186-9. — ISBN 0-8157-5185-0 (pbk.)
    1. Foreign trade and employment. 2. Labor market.
3. International trade. 4. Unemployment. 5. Foreign trade
and employment—United States.
I. Title.
HD5710.7.L393   1996
382'.3—dc20   96-25252
                                                            CIP

9 8 7 6 5 4 3 2 1

The paper used in this publication meets the minimum requirements of the
American National Standard for Information Sciences—Permanence of Paper for
Printed Library Materials, ANSI Z39-48-1984.

Typeset in Times Roman

Composition by Harlowe Typography, Inc.
Cottage City, Maryland

Printed by R. R. Donnelley and Sons Co.
Harrisonburg, Virginia

Acknowledgments

I AM PARTICULARLY grateful to Charles Oman of the OECD Development Centre for his encouragement and many useful comments. I am also grateful to John Martin of the OECD Directorate for Education, Employment, Labour, and Social Affairs for helpful detailed comments on an earlier version, to participants in the Development Centre Seminar of June 1995, and to Nick Vanston and his colleagues in the OECD Economics Department, especially Bénédicte Larre, for their comments and help with data. I have learned much from collaboration in some of this work with Matthew Slaughter and Paul Krugman. I thank Scott Bradford, Carolyn Evans, Eric Pan, and Howard Shatz for research assistance and Howard Shatz, David Weinstein, and Adrian Wood for comments.

—RZL

Preface

THE DETERIORATION of OECD labor markets in recent years has coincided with the rise of globalization and the rapid growth of exports from developing countries. As shown by the 1994 OECD Jobs Study, that deterioration is most visible in high rates of unemployment in Europe, while in the United States, it takes the form of falling real wages for production workers, growing income inequality, and increasing numbers of working poor.

The relationship between globalization and the poor performance of OECD labor markets has become the subject of a heated and divisive policy debate. In addition to globalization and imports from low-wage countries, many blame OECD firms that have relocated to developing countries production destined mainly for OECD markets.

In OECD countries these views contribute to a worrisome increase in protectionist pressures directed against developing countries. Moreover, this is happening at a time when more and more non-OECD countries are finally turning outward, moving to adopt market-friendly policies and seeking to compete in global markets.

This study, undertaken by the Development Centre in conjunction with its research programme on "Globalisation and Competition," seeks to clarify the relationship between OECD countries' trade with developing countries and the performance of OECD labor markets. It concludes that while trade between the two groups of countries has played some role in reducing the relative wages of poorly educated workers in the United States and in raising unemployment in Europe, its impact has been insignificant. Similarly, the international sourcing activities of OECD-based multinational firms have had only a minor impact.

What, then, accounts for the deterioration of OECD labor markets? Throughout the study, the role of technological and organizational change at the level of firms appears preeminent. For example, poor average wage performance in the United States reflects slow productivity growth outside manufacturing—in services, construction, and mining, for instance—while more rapid productivity growth in manufacturing has led to a shedding of labor, particularly workers with low levels of education in that sector. The relative speed of technological change, the "biased" nature of both technological and organizational change as firms move to become more flexible, and market rigidities, notably in Europe, have played a dominant role in OECD labor-market performance.

Resistance to these changes through trade protection is not the answer. Rather, the major challenges are in the realm of domestic policy. The study recommends that OECD countries educate voters on the sources of the problem; introduce measures, such as earned-income tax credits, which redress earnings inequality while preserving or increasing the flexibility of wages and markets; and promote organizational change and improved public and private systems of education and training, which, by reducing both market and firm-level rigidities, help more firms and workers to take advantage of opportunities offered by the new technologies.

The study, written by one of the world's top international economists, contributes to a better understanding of the relationship between globalization and the poor performance of OECD labor markets. Highly policy relevant, it sheds important light on the value of maintaining, indeed strengthening, an open global trading system.

The OECD Development Centre is very pleased to publish this important study jointly with the Brookings Institution Press.

JEAN BONVIN
President

OECD Development Centre
July 1996

Contents

Figures

Introduction

THE PAST DECADE has witnessed some miraculous changes in the world economy. Particularly noteworthy have been those in the developing and former communist nations. Since the mid-1980s developing countries throughout the world have turned away from protectionist and statist policies and embraced outwardly oriented policies. Privatization and trade liberalization are the order of the day. China, the world's most populous country, has enjoyed the most rapid growth by embracing a strategy of export-led growth driven by foreign investment. Many other nations in Asia, Latin America, and even Africa are adopting similar strategies. The former planned economies of eastern Europe and the Soviet Union are emerging from an economically disastrous half-century and embracing capitalism. All are counting on being able to reap the benefits of international integration.

By contrast, the early 1990s witnessed a recession in the developed economies. By the mid-1990s, in most developed economies, cyclical recovery had taken hold, but reduced labor-force growth and slower productivity growth have decreased the potential growth rates projected for the second half of the decade. With slow growth at home, the dynamic emerging markets in the developing world offer particularly attractive opportunities. In principle, therefore, a liberal international trade and investment order should provide significant opportunities for mutual gains.

An important question, however, is whether this process will be allowed to occur: in particular, whether the developed countries will be able to keep their markets open and make the necessary adjustments to absorb developing-country exports. That will not be easy. For two decades labor-market performance in the developed world has been less than

1

Table I-1. *Percent Change in Mean Earnings of Full-Time Workers in the United States, 1980–90*

Category	All	Male	Female
Managers	75	78	88
Technical	72	66	74
Service	65	60	68
Precision	54	55	62
Farm	53	53	58
Operators	51	48	56
College plus	83	85	91
College	72	69	92
High school	57	52	71
High school minus	40	38	52

Source: CPS tapes.

satisfactory. In the United States real wages have stagnated and relative wages have become more dispersed. In Europe unemployment, especially among low-wage workers, has increased dramatically.

In 1973, measured in 1982 dollars, the hourly earnings of nonsupervisory workers in the United States were $8.55. By 1994 they had *declined* to $7.40, a level that had been achieved in the mid-1960s. Had earnings increased at their earlier pace, they would have been well over $12. Or consider real hourly compensation, a more comprehensive measure of the payments to labor because it includes fringe benefits as well as earnings. Between 1973 and 1994 real hourly compensation rose by only 9 percent.

A second ominous development in the American economy has accompanied this decline in real earnings: a dramatic increase in the inequality of earnings based on education and occupation. Table I-1 reports changes in the weekly earnings of full-time workers by education, occupation, and gender, derived from the Current Population Survey tapes of 1980 and 1990. The story it reveals is striking. When ranged by education or occupation, the changes over the decade have an uninterrupted pattern: the higher the level of education, the higher the increase in earnings. The premium commanded by both men and women with higher educational or occupational status has notably increased. American men with more than a college degree who were employed full time saw their nominal earnings rise by 83 percent, but those with less than a high-school degree experienced only a 40 percent increase, falling behind the rise in the U.S. consumer price index, which grew by 58.6 percent over the decade. Similarly, the earnings of managers rose 75 percent, while all blue-collar occupations failed to keep pace with inflation, the worst off being operators, whose nominal earnings increased by just 51 percent.[1] American women tended to do better than their male counterparts, but their improvement was also related to education and occupation.[2] However one distinguishes the skilled from the unskilled, the sharp rise in wage inequality between the two in the 1980s is clear.[3]

Growing inequality is also evident in the United Kingdom. According to the Organization for Economic Cooperation and Development (OECD), in the United Kingdom there was a substantial increase in the ratio of earnings of the highest (90th) to lowest (10th) percentile.[4] According to Stephen Machin, between 1975 and 1990 the ratio of nonmanual to manual wages increased from 1.31 to 1.50, a marked reversal of the downward trend that had prevailed over the postwar period.[5] But in the United Kingdom, unlike in the United States, the real wages of the lowest decile rose.[6]

By contrast with the United States and the United Kingdom, continental Europe's poor labor-market performance was not evident in its wage behavior. In continental European countries during the 1980s, real wages typically *grew* by 1 to 2 percent annually. Moreover, wage differentials either were broadly unchanged or increased only slightly. An important issue in Europe, however, is the degree to which institutional and regulatory factors repressed wage adjustments and raised unemploy-

1. Bound and Johnson (1992) found that between 1979 and 1988 the ratio of the average wage of a college graduate to the average wage of a high-school graduate rose by 15 percent. Davis (1992) found that between 1979 and 1987 the ratio of weekly earnings of males in their forties to weekly earnings of males in their twenties rose by 25 percent.

2. The employment cost index shows that between December 1979 and December 1992 the growth of compensation and earnings of white-collar occupations exceeded those of blue-collar occupations by 7.9 and 10.9 percent, respectively.

3. In addition to the increase in inequality when workers are grouped by these characteristics, there has been a considerable increase in inequality that is unexplained by the measured skills of the workers. Juhn, Murphy, and Pierce (1993). Also, Freeman (forthcoming) points out that despite the huge drop in the relative pay of less-skilled workers in the United States, their relative employment rates deteriorated and their relative unemployment rates failed to improve.

4. OECD (1993).

5. Machin (1994, p. 21). In 1955 the ratio was 1.40.

6. In Canada and Australia, as in the United States, low-paid workers experienced real wage declines. But the rise in inequality was much less marked. Freeman (1991) and Katz, Loveman, and Blanchflower (1992) find increasing education and age differentials in those countries but to a much smaller degree than in the United States. Fahrer and Pease (1994) find that in Australia the relative wages of unskilled workers have not fallen.

ment.[7] Indeed, since 1973 almost all European countries have experienced high levels of unemployment, particularly of younger workers and those out of work for more than twelve months.[8] In 1993, for example, such workers accounted for fewer than 12 percent of the unemployed in the United States, but in Germany, France, the United Kingdom, and Italy, the share ranged between 34 and 58 percent. In addition, as noted by Richard Freeman, the ratio of employment to the population of working age and hours worked per employee in Europe relative to that in the United States has trended down since the 1970s.[9]

In summarizing this experience, therefore, the OECD *Jobs Study* concludes that all countries have experienced a shift in demand away from unskilled jobs. In countries where relative wages have been flexible, both relative employment and unemployment rates of the unskilled changed little during the 1980s. In countries with less wage flexibility, the effects have been felt by a deterioration in the employment and unemployment performance of the unskilled.[10]

The Role of International Factors

In both Europe and the United States, alarms have been sounded about the role of trade and international investment in shifting the demand for unskilled labor. As regards the United States, the fact that its changed international economic relations have coincided with slow real wage growth and widening wage inequality makes it scarcely surprising that the former has frequently been advanced as a primary cause of the latter. The two developments—sluggish and unequal real-wage growth—

7. OECD (1993) notes that those countries which did not experience an increase in dispersion over the 1980s—Denmark, Finland, Germany, Italy, and Norway—are countries where national institutions have a particularly strong influence on wage setting.

8. See OECD (1994).

9. Freeman (forthcoming). Also striking in both Europe and the United States has been the relative decline in the employment of manual workers in industry in general and manufacturing in particular. EuroStat data indicate that between 1978 and 1988 the decline in the ratio of industrial employment of manual to nonmanual workers in Germany (− 16.1 percent) and Ireland (− 15.1 percent) was similar to the decline in the ratio of production to nonproduction workers in United States manufacturing (− 18.5 percent), while declines (in the ratio of manual to nonmanual workers) were about twice as large in French (− 26.8 percent), Danish (− 27.7 percent), and Italian (− 30.4 percent) manufacturing. The data suggest (a) a universal decline in the demand for production workers and (b) a trade-off between wage flexibility and employment opportunities.

10. For a more extensive discussion, see Freeman and Katz (1994).

occurred at the same time as three major changes in U.S. international economic relations.

The first was convergence: the change in America's comparative position from global economic preeminence to "first among equals." In the 1950s output per worker in America was twice that in western Europe and six times that in Japan. Today Europe and Japan have closed most of the output gap.[11] In addition, since the 1950s both human capital and physical capital have been growing more rapidly in foreign industrialized countries than in the United States. The result has been a convergence in wage rates. In 1975 a trade-weighted average of foreign compensation rates expressed in U.S. dollars was equal to 64 percent of the average U.S. level. By 1980 this measure stood at 72 percent, and by 1990, 93 percent.[12]

The second major change was globalization: the increased volume of foreign trade and foreign direct investment in the United States. Between 1970 and 1990 U.S. exports plus imports as a percentage of gross national product rose from 12.7 to 24.9 percent. During the 1980s the ratio of the stock of inward foreign direct investment to GNP, valued on a historic cost basis, grew from 3.0 to 8.1 percent.[13] Since the first oil shock in 1973, Americans have been forced to adjust to foreigners as suppliers of raw materials, as competitors in manufactures (such as automobiles), and finally as bankers and bosses.

The third major change was spending: the shift in American spending patterns in the 1980s that produced record trade deficits. The Reagan administration's combination of expansionary fiscal policy and contractionary monetary policy helped cause an unprecedented appreciation of the U.S. dollar until 1985. This record strength of the dollar priced many American exporters out of the world market, and it made imports a bargain for American consumers. The result was an enormous growth in the trade deficit: from 0.5 percent of gross domestic product in 1980 to nearly 3.5 percent of GDP in 1987.[14]

11. McKinsey (1992).

12. This measure includes twenty-four U.S. trading partners; it excludes Brazil, Mexico, and Israel. When these countries are included, the 1990 trade-weighted foreign manufacturing compensation measure equals 88 percent of America's. Data come from BLS (1991).

13. United States Council of Economic Advisers (1995).

14. A fourth change has been increased immigration. As noted by Freeman (forthcoming), in the 1970 census of population 4.7 percent of the U.S. population was born overseas. In the 1990 census the number was 7.9 percent. Moreover, most recent immigrants have come from developing countries.

In the United States the debate over the North American Free Trade Agreement in the early 1990s crystallized concerns about the role of international factors in wage performance. These were best captured by Ross Perot's allusion to the "giant sucking sound" of jobs as they move southward. Another concern was the impetus NAFTA would provide for what many in the United States see as a serious problem: "runaway plants," or the relocation by multinationals to low-wage countries. Despite the passage of NAFTA many Americans continue to worry about these issues. During the 1996 presidential campaign, Patrick Buchanan called for the repeal of NAFTA and the imposition of a tariff to offset lower Mexican wages.

In Europe the absorption into the European Community of low-wage countries like Spain and Portugal proceeded fairly smoothly during the growth phase in the late 1980s. The recessionary environment of the 1990s, however, has sparked fears of "delocalization," namely, that firms are relocating to low-wage countries.[15] In France, in a best-selling book, Sir James Goldsmith voiced apprehension about trade and immigration, and the French Senate issued a special report blaming delocalization for many of France's ills.[16] These concerns have become particularly important as eastern European nations seek full membership in the European Union.

In Japan, where the expressed concern is about the hollowing out of the Japanese economy, the debate over globalization has become heated in recent years. The strengthening of the yen in the mid-1980s initiated this concern as Japanese manufacturers began to invest outside Japan in increasing numbers. After a period of respite in which a booming domestic economy laid some of the fears to rest, the association of slow growth and a strong yen have again brought them to the fore. As Japanese firms increasingly relocate abroad, many question whether Japanese manufacturers can continue to maintain their basic institutions such as lifetime employment and strong corporate groups.

Further, many countries have voiced concern about international competition in the labor market with regard not only to wages but also to the regulatory environment that governs employment. In Canada some have seen free trade with the United States as a threat to Canada's welfare state. In Europe an important aspect of creating the single market

15. Buiges and Jacquemin (1994).
16. Goldsmith (1993); Arthuis (1993).

has been the "social dimension," the effort to ensure that minimum social standards prevail throughout the European Union. In France a furor arose when the Hoover Corporation moved from Dijon to Scotland, purportedly attracted by both lower wage costs and lower labor standards. In the European debate about freer trade with eastern Europe and Asia, many have expressed concern not simply about low wages but about "social dumping," the downward competitive pressure that is allegedly placed on labor standards as a result of trade. In the United States concern about worker rights has increasingly been reflected in U.S. international trade legislation. Indeed, both France and the United States have proposed that worker rights be placed high on the post-Uruguay Round agenda of multilateral trade negotiations.

Labor Pauperization

There are both spurious and serious theories linking trade and poor wage performance. The most common claim that trade with developing countries has an adverse impact on living standards in developed countries rests on a proposition that seems to be grounded in common sense; namely, that high-wage countries cannot compete with low-wage countries. If workers are paid $15 a hour in the United States and just $2 dollars an hour in Mexico, no one will produce anything in the United States. But this proposition is fundamentally flawed; it assumes that international competitiveness depends only on relative wages. But what matters in international competition are relative *costs*, not just relative wages and other factor prices. If workers are more productive in the United States because the United States has superior knowhow, a better infrastructure, or a larger capital stock, this superior productivity can offset higher U.S. wages in determining costs. The more sophisticated modern proponents of this "labor pauperization" argument acknowledge the validity of this point but suggest that today, unlike in earlier times, capital, technology, and entrepreneurship are all internationally mobile. According to Klaus Schwab and Claude Smadja, for example, "the whole phenomenon of delocalization has broken the linkage that previously existed among high technology, high productivity, high quality, and high wages. It was this linkage that once appeared to guarantee ever improving standards of living in industrialized countries. Today, however, it is possible to have high technology, high productivity, high quality and *low wages*."[17]

The central assumption there is that low-wage workers in developing countries are just as productive as workers in developed countries. According to this view, firms producing in developing countries will have lower costs *no matter what they choose to produce. In other words, developing countries will have an advantage in producing everything.* Under these circumstances developed countries will be unable to compete, and developed-country workers face dismal prospects. Either they must find employment in the segments of the service economy that must be provided locally—although these sectors are dwindling because of improvements in telecommunications—or they must accept lower wages or face unemployment.

Proponents of this modern pauperization view take a valid observation and exaggerate its consequences. It is true that as technology and capital become more mobile, comparative advantage can shift. *In some industries*, therefore, developed countries will indeed experience an erosion in comparative advantage. But this will not be true of all industries. Some processes and technologies can be moved internationally, but the most significant sources of higher productivity in the developed countries—the superior levels of skills and the tacit knowledge of the work force—cannot move abroad, because they are firmly planted in the hands and brains of developed-country workers. Similarly, vital aspects of social capital are embodied in the culture, in formal institutions, and in informal relationships and networks that remain location specific. Finally, infrastructure, communications, and other forms of physical capital remain far superior in developed countries.

Both the naive and the modern proponents of these labor-pauperization views fail to understand David Ricardo's basic insight, that trade is driven by comparative rather than absolute advantage. Countries will gain from trade as long as their domestic relative cost structures differ from international prices. The same process that decreases comparative advantage in some sectors automatically increases it in others. When international competitive pressures cause a contraction in sectors competing with imports, this simultaneously makes more resources available for export industries.

17. Schwab and Smadja (1994, p. 41).

Multinational companies, improved communications, and other factors have diffused knowhow internationally, allowing developing countries to specialize in products such as textiles, electronics, footwear, and toys. That may indeed mean more competition in these industries for firms in developed countries. But this competition is not the end of the story. Consumers in developed countries benefit because they can buy such products more cheaply. Producers also benefit because developing countries typically spend the money they earn by buying sophisticated manufactured products such as chemicals, computers, and machinery from the developed countries.

Notwithstanding the logic of the theory of comparative advantage, the labor-pauperization view has widespread appeal because it appears to explain the facts. The poor wage performance in the United States and high unemployment in Europe seem to confirm the predictions of such a view. But before these problems are ascribed to the modern pauperization hypothesis, the absence of a critical corollary must be explained: namely, why are developing countries poor? Output is by definition the sum of wages plus profits and rents. If output per worker is actually the same throughout the world economy, while wages per worker are much lower, profits and rents per worker in the developing world should be enormous; in fact, total national income per worker should be the same in developed and developing economies. But that is not the case. Indeed, measured in U.S. dollars, output per worker in the foreign affiliates of American companies in developed countries is more than two and a half times higher than in their affiliates in developing countries.[18] The fact that output per worker is not similar worldwide indicates that not all sources of international competitive advantage are readily mobile.

Alternative Theories

There are other, more solidly grounded theories linking trade and wages. Some of these theories assume that markets are competitive and factors of production mobile; others assume imperfect competition and specific factors. I consider each of these in turn.

18. See table 5-3 in chapter 5.

Competitive Markets

Although the theory of international trade suggests that free trade will raise national income, it does not suggest that all factors of production will share equally in those gains. If a nation begins to trade, it will specialize in the production of goods it can make relatively cheaply. Compared with no trade, therefore, trade will raise the relative price of exported products and lower the relative price of imported products. One would thus expect that the factor of production that is more important in export industries would gain, while the factor that is more important in the import-competing sector would gain less (or lose). In fact, Wolfgang Stolper and Paul Samuelson showed how an increase in trade through the removal of import barriers would raise the real return of the factor used relatively intensively in the production of exports but actually lower, in absolute terms, the return to the factor of production used relatively intensively in the production of imported products.[19] If developed-country imports are produced using unskilled labor relatively intensively, therefore, freer trade with the emerging economies could reduce the wages of unskilled workers while raising the wages of skilled workers.

Trade theory also suggests that trade could equalize wages and other factor prices around the world—the factor-price-equalization theorem. Indeed, trade could actually substitute for factor mobility. Just as the free international movement of labor and capital would equalize wages and profits globally, so too would free trade. But for this result to obtain, two conditions are necessary. First, technological capabilities must be similar throughout the world, and second, there should be sufficient overlap in the products all countries produce. However, even if these conditions were satisfied, the crucial question is whether the result would be lower wages in the developed world or higher wages in the developing world. By and large, since the driving force is the international diffusion of technology—that is, improving productivity in the developing countries—the equalization process occurs through a leveling up rather than

---

19. Stolper and Samuelson (1941). At one level this result seems obvious. If a country specializes in exporting labor-intensive products, one would expect labor to derive unusually large benefits. The surprising result, however, is that labor gets more than all the gains from trade, and the factor used relatively less intensively is actually hurt by trade. It should also be emphasized that this result depends critically on the absence of economies of scale.

a leveling down. As developing countries acquire the skills, technology, and capital levels of the developed countries, they converge toward developed-country wages.

In principle, these theoretical issues were, of course, highly relevant to the United States in the immediate postwar period, when the United States was globally preeminent. Over that golden era (1950–73), the U.S. economy reduced its trade barriers and expanded its trade with "low-wage" nations in Europe and Japan, and the world economy achieved significant wage convergence among developed countries. The Stolper-Samuelson theory did not excite much attention among U.S. policymakers because real wages in the United States rose steadily, and wage differentials between skilled and unskilled workers actually narrowed. Indeed, over the 1970s, although the U.S. economy became considerably more open—trade doubled as a share of GNP—the premium earned by educated workers declined.

The factor-price-equalization theorem provided better predictions. As Europe and Japan joined the United States on the technological frontier, their wage rates converged toward (and in some cases surpassed) those in the United States. But since convergence involved a leveling-up process, in which wages in other developed countries rose to U.S. levels, the process was viewed as fairly benign. (Although some viewed America as "in decline," this related to its relative rather than to its absolute income level.) Today, however, as I analyze in this study, these theories are seen as having more ominous implications. There are economists who ascribe the poor labor-market performance of unskilled workers in the developed countries to the Stolper-Samuelson process,[20] and others who invoke the factor-price-equalization theorem to argue that international wages will converge through downward adjustments in the developed countries.[21]

Premium Wages and Rents

The Stolper-Samuelson perspective assumes that the world is characterized by perfectly competitive markets, homogeneous factors of production, and constant returns to scale. It implies that similar workers earn the same wages regardless of the industry in which they are employed. In reality, some industries pay higher wages than others, even

20. Wood (1994).
21. Leamer (1991).

when workers have similar qualifications.[22] To explain such behavior, it is necessary to use theoretical paradigms that make the more realistic assumption that international markets are not perfectly competitive. Under these circumstances, particular firms and factors may earn premiums or rents. One source of these rents is innovation. Firms with new inventions or products earn supernormal profits until they are emulated. Another source is market power. Firms with monopolies may also earn premium profits. Similarly, trade unions with such power in the labor market may gain premium wages for their members. Heavily concentrated and highly unionized industries often yield both premium profits and premium wages.

Increased international competition could affect these premiums and rents. Indeed, one view is that the slow U.S. real wage growth reflects an erosion in the rents the United States once earned from its technological leadership.[23] A second view is that increased trade penetration and the increased possibility of sourcing products internationally has put downward pressure on the wages unionized workers can demand.[24] A third view is that international competition has reduced the size of the manufacturing sector and thus shrunk the availability of premium-wage manufacturing jobs; this view is sometimes termed deindustrialization.

To account for the channels by which international forces may affect the labor market, therefore, both types of hypotheses should be considered: those emphasizing international pressures resulting from competitive product and factor markets and those emphasizing changes in premiums and rents. In this study, I pay attention to both.

Before proceeding, however, I should emphasize that globalization has clearly not been the only factor responsible for the labor-market performance. In particular, domestic forces have played an important role. Technological change and change in corporate organizational structures (for example, the move to a lean or other more flexible form of organization) have shifted the demand for different types of labor. Domestic demand has induced shifts in sectoral employment. Institutional changes such as the role of unions, and government policies such as minimum wages and demographic factors, all play a role. It lies beyond the scope of this study to provide a full account of the relative importance of this multiplicity of factors. Instead, my aim is to concentrate on the impact

22. Katz and Summers (1989).
23. Johnson and Stafford (1993).
24. Borjas and Ramey (1993).

Figure I-1. *Shares of Manufactured Imports from Developing Countries in the Apparent Consumption of the European Community, the United States, and Japan, 1968–89*

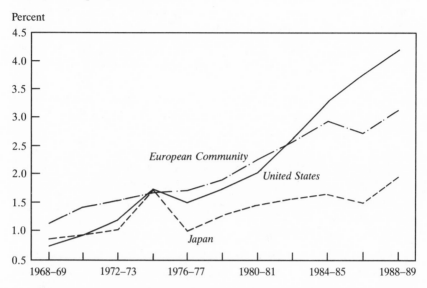

Percent

Source: UNCTAD, *Handbook of International Trade and Development Statistics*, 1992.

of trade in general and trade with developing countries in particular. But I suggest that the incidence of technological and organizational change has been of great importance.

Outline of the Study

For several reasons the U.S. experience is particularly useful for a detailed analysis of the role of trade. First, U.S. wages are generally more flexible than those in other countries. Thus if trade is having a major impact on the labor market, it might be expected to show up first in the U.S. data. Second, the United States, as the most productive large industrial economy, is likely to be most vulnerable if, in fact, international disparities in wage rates lead to lower wages in leading countries. Third, the United States has been more open to trade with developing countries than either Europe or Japan. As indicated in figure I-1, compared with the shares of the European Community and Japan, the U.S. share of apparent consumption of manufactured goods imported from developing countries was higher and rose more rapidly over the 1980s. Fourth, the United States remains the world's largest multinational investor. American multinational firms span the globe, and if developments within these corporations affect domestic labor markets, again the United States will be the most susceptible. For these reasons, therefore, while I introduce evidence from other OECD economies, I pay special attention to the U.S. economy.

Chapter 1 therefore concentrates on a particularly American issue: the impact of trade on *average* U.S. wage behavior. Thereafter the study turns to the issue of *relative* wage behavior in the OECD. Chapter 2 summarizes and evaluates studies that estimate the net-factor content of trade to discern the links between trade and wages. Chapter 3 presents an international analysis based on price evidence and an account of U.S. relative wage behavior based on domestic technological change. Chapter 4 examines the effect of trade on premium wages. Chapter 5 looks at evidence on wages and employment in multinationals both at home and abroad. Chapter 6 considers future prospects, exploring a scenario in which U.S. manufactured goods trade with developing countries expands to five times its current volume. And finally, chapter 7 discusses policy and presents some conclusions.

The central conclusion of the study is that while trade has had some part in reducing the relative wages of poorly educated workers in the United States and in raising the unemployment of unskilled workers in Europe, its impact has been small compared with that of other factors. Moreover, the impact of trade with developing countries on economywide wage trends is also likely to be relatively small in the future. There is little support for those positions that ascribe a major role in this story to expanding trade. There is some evidence in the net-factor-content studies that in the 1980s trade has had small negative effects on the relative wages of unskilled workers, but little evidence in studies that use price approaches, and there is very limited evidence of negative effects on relative industry wages, which operate by reducing the levels of wage premiums or the numbers of workers earning them. None of these findings are large enough to account for a substantial share of the deteriorating relative condition of less-skilled workers. Similarly, the international sourcing activities of multinational corporations have increased rapidly but continue to account for a small share of their overall domestic sales. In addition, multinationals play a small role in employment in developing countries, and their foreign operations in developing countries remain small compared with their domestic employment. Although a large increase in trade with developing countries in the next few decades could further increase relative wage inequality, the magnitude of the relative shift is likely to be fairly small. Likewise, such trade could reduce the real wages of unskilled workers, but by considerably less than 5 percent. And once the process of adjusting to new patterns of specialization is complete, the real wages of unskilled workers are likely to rise.

If trade does not account for wage performance, what does? Throughout this study the impact of domestic technological and organizational change appears to be preeminent. Poor average wage performance in the United States reflects slow U.S. productivity growth outside manufacturing, primarily in such sectors as services, finance, construction, and mining. The relatively rapid productivity growth in U.S. manufacturing—and it is only rapid compared with nonmanufacturing—has led to the shedding of labor in manufacturing, particularly of workers with low levels of education. In addition and most important, production methods in manufacturing and elsewhere have shifted at a rapid pace toward the use of educated, white-collar workers and away from less-educated, blue-collar workers. Both the fairly rapid technological and organizational change and the biased nature of that change have played a dominant role in reducing the wages of less-educated U.S. workers. These are not changes that will be or could be eradicated by trade protection or changes in worker standards. Increased trade protection could perhaps be used to provide one-time relief to the less-skilled domestic workers, but even if the developed economies were reduced to autarky, domestic technological change would continue, creating the same pressures. Policies would do better to focus on two things: first, on improving worker training and education and otherwise promoting and facilitating firms' and workers' adaptation to technological and organizational change and second, on compensating the less fortunate through transfer mechanisms that do not distort incentives to hire or work.

CHAPTER ONE

The End of the American Dream

For a hundred years, between the 1870s and the 1970s, output per worker in the United States increased at an annual rate of just under 2 percent a year. Reflecting this rise in productivity, average real wages increased at a similar pace. This 2 percent pace meant that real wages doubled every thirty-five years, making the American Dream a reality: each successive generation lived twice as well as its predecessor. Since 1973 the dream no longer holds. Real wage growth in the United States has departed sharply from its long-run trend. Between 1973 and 1994 real compensation increased by just 8.6 percent—less than half a percent a year. Not only was the rise in compensation slow, but it lagged considerably behind the 24 percent rise in output per hour recorded over the same period.

Many view those data as a confirmation that international factors have hurt American workers. One argument places the blame on America's relative decline. George Johnson and Frank Stafford argue that the erosion of high returns from American technological leadership has been the principal source of the slow rise in American real wages since 1973.[1] A second argument is that international trade has led to "factor-price equalization," in which American wage rates decline to levels in other countries.[2] A third, less technical but more popular, view is simply that

1. Johnson and Stafford (1992).
2. See Leamer (1991).

16

the combination of international competition and corporate downsizing has put labor on the retreat, giving the upper hand to employers. Indeed, this view has been reinforced by the coincidence of press reports of slow wage growth and record profits and stock prices. Finally, another more popular argument is that high-wage jobs in manufacturing have disappeared; in particular, that "deindustrialization" due to poor U.S. competitive performance in manufacturing is to blame for the poor wage performance.

A careful reading of the data, however, supports none of these views. In this chapter I show that the slowdown in real U.S. wage growth was generated in America and is not the result of international factors. Since the mid-1970s trade has played only a modest role in the declining share of U.S. manufacturing employment, a decline that, in any case, is too small to have had a large impact on average wages in the economy as a whole. Over this period American wages have also not been depressed by the erosion of U.S. technological leadership or by pressures leading to factor-price equalization or a submissive labor force. The problem of slow American wage growth does not reflect the fact that either foreigners or capitalists have taken a bigger share of the pie. Instead, it results from the fact that the pie itself has only grown slowly. The slow growth reflects a decline in U.S. productivity growth, primarily in the sectors of the U.S. economy not heavily involved in international trade; that is, those outside manufacturing. I also provide evidence that much of the real wage growth in other major industrial nations, except for the United Kingdom, is being driven by sustained improvements in productivity growth outside manufacturing. The dominant source of the convergence of wages in the developed countries toward U.S. wage levels is thus differences in productivity growth in services rather than differences in trade performance.

Before I explain average U.S. wage behavior, it is necessary to clarify how wages are measured. The most commonly cited statistic—real average hourly earnings of production workers—shows a *decline* of almost 15 percent between 1973 and 1994. By contrast, a second commonly cited series—real hourly compensation in the business sector—shows an *increase* of 8.6 percent over the same period. These series differ for two reasons: first, the average hourly earnings series samples only production or nonsupervisory workers, while the hourly compensation series includes all persons engaged in work (including the self-employed); second, the hourly earnings series reflects only wages, while the compensation measure includes employers' contributions for social insurance and private benefit plans (including retirement and medical care). Both differences are important, and the series have diverged because (a) the wages of production workers have risen more slowly than those of nonproduction workers, and (b) for all workers, fringe benefits have increased more rapidly than wages. The rest of the chapter focuses on the aggregate compensation measure, because of its broader coverage of the work force and its inclusion of fringe benefits.

Between 1973 and 1979 real compensation in the United States increased slowly, by just 4 percent. But this rise was virtually the same as the 4.6 percent total increase in output per hour. Slower productivity growth therefore explains compensation. The puzzle arises in the period after 1979, in which productivity growth seems to have outstripped real wage growth; thus the post-1979 experience is the focus of my analysis.

Assessing Compensation Performance

From a theoretical standpoint, compensation rather than earnings is the relevant measure of "wages" on which one should focus. One expects workers to be hired as long as their compensation cost is less than their marginal revenue product. As a first approximation, one also expects changes in real compensation to match the change in output per worker. Consider what occurred in the United States.

Since the growth of output per worker in the United States did slow down dramatically after 1973, it is reasonable to expect that real compensation would decline in parallel. A casual inspection of the data suggests, however, that real compensation failed to match even the slow improvement in average labor productivity growth. As figure 1-1 shows, between 1973 and 1979 average real compensation (average hourly compensation deflated by the consumer price index for urban consumers [CPI-U]) increased in line with output per hour in the U.S. business sector. By contrast, from 1979 to 1994 the two trends diverged markedly. Whereas output per worker grew by 18.4 percent—already a very slow pace by historical standards—real hourly compensation grew by only 4.4 percent.

If workers have not seen their real incomes rise as rapidly as output per worker, it is natural to assume that someone else has received this discrepancy. One candidate is owners of capital; a second is foreigners. Indeed, the decade of greed and the impact of international convergence

Figure 1-1. *Output per Hour and Compensation, United States, 1970–94*[a]

1979 = 100

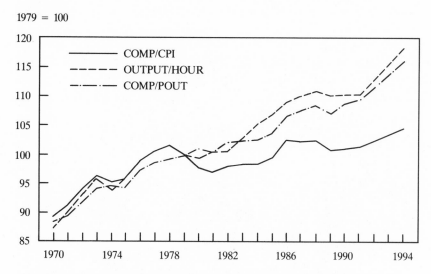

Source: United States Council of Economic Advisers, *Economic Report of the President, 1996*, table B-45.
[a]COMP/CPI is average real compensation deflated by the consumer price index for urban consumers. OUTPUT/ HOUR is output per hour in the business sector. COMP/POUT is average real compensation deflated by the deflator for output.

both in reducing U.S. buying power and in shifting income away from labor have been cited as explanations of the output-wage gap.[3]

These explanations can be rejected, however, in favor of a more straightforward one that involves the basket of goods that workers consume. The index used in calculating real compensation, the CPI, measures a basket of consumption goods typically consumed in the United States and not the basket that workers produce. It follows that nominal compensation deflated by the CPI does not equal nominal compensation deflated by a basket of production goods. If one deflates nominal compensation by the output deflator used in the business-output measures of productivity, one finds that between 1979 and 1994 real product compensation actually increased by 16 percent—just 2.4 percent less than the increase in output per worker (see table 1-1). Thus if wages are deflated with the prices appropriate for measuring the product wage, the output-wage gap virtually disappears.

3. See, for example, Krugman (1992) on greed; Johnson and Stafford (1992) on reducing U.S. buying power; Leamer (1991) on shifting income from labor.

Table 1-1. *Earnings Evaluated by Different Measures, 1970–94*
1979 = 100

Year	Earnings /CPI	Comp /CPI	Output per hour	Comp /POut	Comp /POut-I	Comp/ CPI-Sh	FWTOT	CompShare	GDP87/ hours
1970	98.0	89.4	87.5	88.5	86.1	88.1	126.5	67.0	89.3
1971	100.4	91.2	90.4	89.7	86.9	89.8	124.2	65.7	92.5
1972	104.3	93.9	93.2	91.8	89.4	92.7	120.0	65.2	93.9
1973	104.5	96.1	95.6	94.0	91.6	94.4	116.9	65.1	95.4
1974	101.4	95.1	93.9	94.3	92.0	93.2	107.1	66.5	94.7
1975	99.1	95.8	96.0	94.3	92.9	94.1	106.9	65.0	97.9
1976	100.7	98.8	98.8	97.3	96.0	96.9	107.3	65.2	100.0
1977	102.1	100.3	100.5	98.7	98.0	98.4	103.8	65.0	100.7
1978	102.7	101.4	101.1	99.4	99.2	100.3	102.0	65.1	100.6
1979	100.0	100.0	100.0	100.0	100.0	100.0	100.0	66.2	100.0
1980	95.2	97.5	99.3	101.0	100.8	99.2	91.7	67.3	100.4
1981	93.9	96.8	100.5	100.4	101.0	98.9	93.9	66.1	101.5
1982	93.8	98.0	100.7	102.1	102.1	100.6	97.6	67.1	101.8
1983	94.9	98.5	102.9	102.4	101.1	100.5	101.5	65.9	103.9
1984	94.3	98.4	105.3	102.6	101.5	100.7	104.4	64.5	104.4
1985	93.8	99.3	106.8	103.7	101.9	102.2	105.7	64.3	105.4
1986	94.1	102.4	109.0	106.6	104.7	106.2	107.6	64.7	107.8
1987	93.2	102.3	110.1	107.5	105.4	106.4	102.5	64.6	107.8
1988	92.4	102.4	111.1	108.2	105.9	106.8	102.7	64.5	108.4
1989	91.8	101.0	110.2	107.1	104.5	105.3	102.0	64.3	108.4
1990	90.3	101.1	110.5	108.8	105.6	105.4	100.2	65.2	109.2
1991	89.4	101.4	110.5	109.5	105.1	105.8	101.5	65.6	110.4
1994	88.8	104.4	118.4	116.0	n.a.	n.a.	103.3	64.5	n.a.

Source: Bureau of Labor Statistics; United States Council of Economic Advisers (1995); U.S. Department of Commerce Bureau of Economic Analysis.

n.a. Not available.

a. Earnings = average hourly earnings, CPI = CPI for all urban consumers; Comp = average hourly compensation; CPI-Sh = CPI minus shelter component; CompShare = share of compensation in business output value-added; output = business sector output (excludes housing); POut = deflator for output; POut-I = deflator for output minus investment; FWTOT = ratio of fixed weight price index of exports of goods and services to price index of imports; Hours = hours worked in business sector.

This means that there has *not* been a major shift in the income of the business sector away from wages and toward profits.[4] Indeed, in 1994 the share of total compensation in the value-added by the business sector was 64.5 percent, only 1.7 percentage points lower than it was in 1979 (see table 1-1).

It is true that in the economic recovery between 1992 and 1995 profits per worker grew more rapidly than average wages. But what is frequently overlooked is that in the slump between 1989 and 1991, it was the reverse—wages grew more rapidly than profits per worker. In fact, in 1995 the share of compensation in corporate sector income was exactly the same as it was in 1989—64.5 percent.

What explains the differences between these output data and the more publicized versions based on household and personal income that indicate growing inequality? As convincingly demonstrated by David Cutler and Lawrence Katz, the discrepancies arise because of data definitions.[5] Unlike personal income data, national income accounts data include in the return to capital both reinvested earnings and taxes on corporate earnings; they exclude capital gains and interest paid on the government debt. The divergence between the output and income measures can be ascribed to these differences. Profits attributable to current earnings on capital, therefore, did not increase dramatically at the expense of compensation.

This explanation of the output-wage gap also means that trade did not *shift income away from labor.* I describe later in greater detail, in the context of a two-factor model, how the traditional Stolper-Samuelson model predicts that changes in the terms of trade reduce the real product return of the factor used intensively in the production of the good whose relative price falls. The finding that real product wages have not fallen and indeed have matched productivity growth is an important piece of evidence that contradicts those who use such a model to argue that the

---

4. Define S as labor's share in income, where W is the nominal compensation rate, L is employment, P is the price of output, and Q is the quantity of output:

$$S = WL/PQ.$$

Expressing both sides in logs, taking the derivative with respect to time and rearranging, one gets

$$S^* = W^* - P^* - (Q^* - L^*).$$

Here $S^* = d\log S/dt$ and so on. So changes in labor's share are equal to the difference between changes in the product wage ($W^* - P^*$), and changes in output per worker ($Q^* - L^*$).

5. Cutler and Katz (1992).

poor U.S. average-wage performance is due to trade's raising the return to capital and lowering the return to labor. If trade had done that, the real product wage would have declined. Instead, it rose by as much as productivity, which means that trade did not have the impact just described.[6]

To summarize, if one deflates nominal compensation by production prices rather than by consumption prices, workers in the 1980s were basically compensated for productivity growth. If workers had chosen to consume the products they produced, they would have raised their real compensation by almost as much as the improvement in productivity growth—16 percent. The wage gap illustrated in figure 1-1 is thus primarily due to a discrepancy between the production and the consumption wage and not to a shift in the distribution of income to capital away from labor. Apparently, the prices of the products that workers consume have risen more rapidly than those that they produce.

Three main differences in the composition of the deflators for production and consumption compensation merit attention. First, the CPI, which is used to measure real consumption earnings, does not, of course, reflect the prices of investment goods. The prices of the most rapidly growing investment goods, computers, have declined precipitously. Simply subtracting gross domestic investment from business-sector output provides a measure of consumption-goods output. The implicit deflator from this series suggests that between 1979 and 1991 real compensation in terms of consumer goods increased by 5.1 percent (versus 1.5 percent using the CPI-U). Thus about half the shortfall between product and consumption compensation can be explained by the relative price decline in investment goods.

A second important compositional difference between the CPI and the business-sector output used in measuring productivity is housing. Output of owner-occupied housing is not included in the business-sector output measure used by the Bureau of Labor Statistics (BLS) to estimate business-sector productivity growth. However, the price of shelter is a

6. Indeed the behavior of the aggregate U.S. business sector between 1979 and 1989 matches the predictions of a conventional neoclassical growth model with pure labor-augmenting technical change. I have already noted that factor shares were constant and that real product compensation rose at the rate of growth of output per worker. I should add that the capital-output ratio remained fairly constant. The growth rates of the net capital stock of fixed nonresidential capital and business-sector output were 31.5 percent and 29.6 percent, respectively. As a result, the 1989 ratio of business-sector profits to net capital stock of 9.1 percent was similar to the 1979 ratio of 8.7 percent.

major component of the consumer price index. Between 1979 and 1991 the index of shelter prices increased 17 percent more rapidly than the rest of the CPI. If one deflates hourly compensation by the CPI minus shelter, one obtains an estimated increase in real compensation between 1979 and 1991 of 5.8 percent—a figure similar to the estimate using the business deflator minus investment goods.

The third main difference between production and consumption prices involves international trade. Imported goods make up part of the consumption basket, but not of the production basket. There is a widespread view that foreign economic growth necessarily increases aggregate U.S. welfare because it provides increased opportunities for trade.[7] However, as Hicks pointed out long ago, this is not necessarily correct.[8] Given domestic output, national welfare depends on the terms of trade, the ratio of export to import prices. Foreign growth *will* raise aggregate U.S. welfare if it improves America's terms of trade by providing either larger markets for U.S. products or cheaper imports, or both. But if growth induced foreigners to boost the output of U.S. exportables (or to shift out of U.S. importables), U.S. welfare could be reduced.[9] In principle, therefore, the sluggish increase in average U.S. real wages could reflect a decline in America's terms of trade.

Given domestic output, real compensation rises when workers must give up fewer resources to obtain a given quantity of imports. Whether real compensation actually rises in this way depends on two factors. The first is the productivity with which factors can be combined to produce domestic products, and the second is the rate at which domestic products can be exchanged for imports—that is, the terms of trade. If the product-wage increase matches domestic productivity growth (as I have just shown it does), the level of real compensation depends on the nation's terms of trade.

Johnson and Stafford have formalized this argument.[10] They describe a model in which U.S. incomes are eroded as developing countries improve their ability to produce medium-technology products in which the United States once specialized. The driving force behind this explanation, however, is the fact that the U.S. terms of trade decline; indeed, it

7. See, for example, Williamson (1991).
8. Hicks (1953).
9. It should be stressed that simply because the gains from trade have been reduced, it does not follow that protection would be a superior policy.
10. Johnson and Stafford (1993).

results from the fact that developing countries produce too few of the goods that are very labor intensive as they move to produce more of the medium-tech goods once produced by the North. In this model the relative price of labor-intensive imports increases more rapidly than that of exports. Table 1-1 reports the fixed-weight measure of the terms of trade over the period of interest. But in contrast to the argument of Johnson and Stafford, this series actually indicates a small *improvement* in the terms of trade. The fixed-weight measure shows an increase of 3.3 percent.[11] Other things equal, these slightly improved terms of trade meant slightly higher real compensation, suggesting that trade raised rather than lowered the buying power of U.S. workers.[12]

Deindustrialization and the Loss of Good Jobs

Table 1-2 reports a variety of measures of the share of manufacturing in the U.S. economy. It is clear that since 1973 the share of manufacturing in overall U.S. employment (and hours worked) has declined even more rapidly than it did earlier. Between 1950 and 1973, for example, the share of manufacturing in total U.S. employment declined by about 1 percent annually. By contrast, between 1973 and 1993 the yearly decline averaged 2.4 percent. However, the claim that the loss of high-wage manufacturing jobs was an important part of the average compensation story can be rejected. Lawrence Katz and Lawrence Summers have estimated the premiums that workers earned in different U.S. industries in 1984.[13] Their estimates of compensation premiums for two-digit manufacturing industries suggest that they averaged 11.8 percent. The share of manufacturing in total U.S. payroll employment declined from 23.8 percent in 1978 to 17.9 percent in 1989. If one assumes that, on average, workers earn no premiums outside manufacturing, as the Katz and Summers

11. As shown in Lawrence (1990), if the prices of computers, oil, and agriculture are excluded, there was virtually no change in the terms of trade for other goods and services between 1980 and 1990.

12. Command GNP differs from conventional GNP in that it deflates nominal exports by the import deflator rather than by the export deflator. If the terms of trade worsen, Command GNP falls relative to GNP, as does America's international buying power. Over the 1980s as a whole, Command GNP actually rose 2 percent more than GNP did.

13. Katz and Summers (1989, p. 298).

Table 1-2. *Manufacturing Share in the U.S. Economy, Selected Years and Periods, 1950–93*

Year	Real GDP (1)	Hours (2)	Employment (3)
1950	n.a.	n.a.	0.337
1960	0.190	0.287	0.310
1973	0.210	0.265	0.262
1977	0.210	n.a.	n.a.
1979	0.207	0.243	0.234
1989	0.197	0.199	0.179
1993	0.187	0.184	0163

	Annual average changes in share				
Period	Real GDP (4)	Hours (5)	Employment (6)	(5) − (4)	(6) − (4)
1960–73	0.768	−0.611	−1.271	−1.379	−2.039
1973–93	−0.578	−1.802	−2.357	−1.224	−1.779
1973–79	−0.214	−1.421	−1.878	−1.208	−1.664
1979–89	−0.497	−1.971	−2.628	−1.474	−2.131
1989–93	−1.323	−1.950	−2.395	−0.628	−1.072

Source: U.S. National Income Accounts.
n.a. Not available.

estimates suggest, then in 1989, had the manufacturing sector retained its 1978 share of U.S. employment at 23.8 percent, average compensation would have been higher by (0.059 × 11.8); that is, seven-tenths of 1 percent. Clearly, therefore, the shift in the composition of employment between manufacturing and services accounts for little of the slow rise in average compensation.

Since trade performance was only one source of the declining share of manufacturing employment—shifts in domestic demand patterns and productivity growth were also important—it is even clearer that poor average U.S. wage performance does not reflect the loss of high-wage manufacturing jobs because of U.S. trade performance.[14] Jeffrey Sachs

14. The relative roles of demand and productivity in manufacturing's declining share are difficult to disentangle because of measurement problems. Measured in 1982 prices, between 1979 and 1989 the volume of manufactured goods produced in the United States increased as rapidly as production in the rest of the economy. Manufacturing output increased by 30.4 percent, while gross national product was up 29 percent. This was sufficient to raise the share of manufacturing value-added in GNP (measured in 1982 dollars) from 22.3 percent in 1979 to 22.6 percent, a share similar to that in 1970 (21.0 percent) and 1960 (20.3 percent). By contrast, 1987 data indicate that between 1979 and 1989 the share of

and Howard Shatz estimate that shifts in international trade between 1978 and 1990 accounted for a net decline equal to 5.9 percent of 1978 manufacturing employment levels.[15] Although this amounts to about 40 percent of the relatively rapid decline in manufacturing employment over the period, the impact of this shift operating through an erosion of high-wage job opportunities is not large enough to have affected aggregate U.S. compensation significantly. Five point nine percent of manufacturing employment in 1978, that is 1.2 million jobs, would equal 6.2 percent of manufacturing employment in 1989. Since manufacturing accounted for 17 percent of total employment in 1989, shifting an additional (0.062 × 17), or 1.05 percent, of employment to manufacturing would have raised average hourly and weekly wages by 0.1 and 0.3 percent, respectively, and economywide wage premiums by 0.12 percent.[16]

A related view, explored in depth in chapter 4, is that international trade has forced the highly unionized manufacturing sector to accept lower rates of compensation. In table 1-3, I report on changes in compensation both inside and outside the manufacturing sector. Over the 1980s average manufacturing compensation increased only 2 percent more slowly than nonmanufacturing. Moreover, between 1990 and 1994 manufacturing compensation actually closed the gap by 1 percent. Thus the evidence does not indicate a major role for either trade or other factors in depressing relative manufacturing compensation.

The relatively rapid decline in the share of U.S. employment in the manufacturing sector since the mid-1970s reflects both U.S. productivity and output growth. In their study of the United Kingdom, Robert Rowthorn and John Wells distinguish between positive and negative deindustrialization. In particular, they define positive deindustrialization as occurring "because productivity growth in the manufacturing sector is so rapid that, despite increasing output, employment in this sector is reduced, either absolutely or as a share of total employment."[17] The productivity data suggest that to some degree the United States has experienced "positive deindustrialization." Rapid productivity growth has

---

manufacturing did decline from 20.7 to 19.7 percent (and even further, to 18.7 percent, by 1993). This share was similar to the 19 percent in 1960 but considerably below the 21 percent share in 1977.

15. Sachs and Shatz (1994).

16. Average hourly earnings in manufacturing were 8.2 percent higher than those in the private sector generally. Average weekly earnings were 29 percent higher and wage premiums, as noted, 11.8 percent higher.

17. Rowthorn and Wells (1987, p. 5).

Table 1-3. *Employment Cost Index in U.S. Private Industry, 1980, 1990, 1994*

December 1980 = 100

Item	1980	1990	1994
Manufacturing			
Compensation	100.0	162.4	189.5
Wages	100.0	154.1	175.3
Benefits	100.0	182.8	224.2
Nonmanufacturing			
Compensation	100.0	166.5	191.0
Wages	100.0	160.3	179.9
Benefits	100.0	184.9	223.7
Ratio of manufacturing to nonmanufacturing			
Compensation	1.00	0.98	0.99
Wages	1.00	0.96	0.97
Benefits	1.00	0.99	1.00

Source: Bureau of Labor Statistics.

meant that output growth in manufacturing has not been associated with much growth in input demand.

It is instructive to separate the role of shifts in demand from that of changes in labor productivity in accounting for the declining share of manufacturing in employment. Productivity measures are not available for the government and nonprofit sector. Therefore, this comparison must use data for the business sector (which is equal to gross domestic product (GDP) minus general government, output of nonprofit institutions, and paid employees of private households).[18]

As seen in table 1-4, both output and productivity played roles in the rapidly declining share of manufacturing in overall U.S. employment from 1973 to 1989. Between 1960 and 1973 the share of manufacturing in business-sector output remained roughly constant—manufacturing output grew slightly more rapidly than the business sector overall—and manufacturing labor productivity growth exceeded that of the rest of the

18. Assembling the data for this exercise is not easy. The United States publishes value-added in 1987 dollars for the business sector going back to the late 1940s. But the series for manufacturing output is available only back to 1987. In addition, because of the rapid decline in computer prices, the measures are highly sensitive to the base year in which the data are expressed. The U.S. Bureau of Labor Statistics does, however, have measures of output and inputs for the business and manufacturing sectors that use a Tornquist output index that is less susceptible to the base-year problem. These data are reported in table 1-3.

Table 1-4. *U.S. Productivity and Output Growth, Selected Years, 1953–89*
1987 = 100

Year or period	Gross output		Hours		Labor productivity		Multifactor productivity	
	All business	*Manufacturing*	*All business*	*Manufacturing*	*All business*	*Manufacturing*	*All business*	*Manufacturing*
1953	33.00	38.10	65.60	94.60	50.30	40.27	65.20	63.50
1960	39.00	40.80	65.40	88.90	59.63	45.89	72.20	68.10
1973	70.10	74.20	80.30	106.60	87.30	69.61	94.20	88.60
1977	77.10	80.10	82.60	102.40	93.34	78.22	96.60	87.30
1979	82.90	85.50	90.10	108.80	92.01	78.58	95.80	88.10
1989	106.80	105.40	106.30	103.50	100.47	101.84	100.80	101.00
Annual average changes in share[a]								
1960–73 (1)	4.61	4.71 (0.09)	1.59	1.41 (−0.18)	2.98	3.26 (0.28)	2.07	2.04 (−0.02)
1973–89 (2)	3.05	2.54 (−0.51)	2.02	−0.21 (−2.23)	1.01	2.76 (1.75)	0.48	0.94 (0.46)
(2) − (1)	...	... (−0.61)	...	... (−2.05)	...	... (1.47)	...	... (0.48)
1953–73 (3)	3.84	3.39 (−0.45)	1.02	0.60 (−0.42)	2.79	2.77 (−0.02)	1.86	1.68 (−0.18)
1973–89 (4)	3.05	2.54 (−0.51)	2.02	−0.21 (−2.23)	1.01	2.76 (1.75)	0.48	0.94 (0.46)
(4) − (3)	...	... (−0.06)	...	... (−1.82)	...	... (1.77)	...	... (0.63)

Source: U.S. Department of Labor, Bureau of Labor Statistics, Multifactor Productivity Estimates.
a. The numbers in parentheses are the differences in column 1 and column 2.

business sector by three-tenths of a percent a year. Thus employment grew slightly slower in manufacturing than in the business sector, that is, by 0.2 percent annually. Between 1973 and 1989, however, the productivity differential widened dramatically. Labor productivity in the entire business sector increased by just 1.0 percent annually, whereas manufacturing labor productivity grew at 2.8 percent. At the same time, annual manufacturing output growth was about half a percent slower than output growth in the business sector as a whole. Thus comparing the two periods 1960–73 and 1973–89 suggests that the slower manufacturing-employment relative growth rate of 2.1 percent a year can be decomposed into a difference of 0.60 percent a year due to slower output growth and 1.5 percent a year due to relatively more rapid growth in manufacturing labor productivity. This implies that trade and other factors influencing demand accounted for a declining employment share of 0.60 percent over fourteen years—that is, 29 percent of the relatively rapid decline in share—while relatively rapid productivity growth accounted for 71 percent. There remains the possibility that some part of the productivity growth was due to trade.

U.S. relative price behavior supports this view of differential productivity growth between manufacturing and the rest of the economy. Though it is difficult to quantify precisely, all the measures shown in figure 1-2 indicate that the decline in relative goods prices was unusually large. For example, in the 1960s and 1970s the GNP deflator for goods declined relative to the overall GNP deflator by 5.0 percent and 5.7 percent, respectively. In the 1980s the decline was 13.1 percent. Similarly, the commodity-price component of the consumer price index declined relative to the services component by 16.2 percent and 13.3 percent, respectively, in the 1960s and 1970s, but by 23.9 percent in the 1980s. And while the producer price index for finished goods actually rose relative to the GNP deflator in the 1970s, it fell by 5.3 percent in the 1960s and by 10.9 percent in the 1980s.[19]

19. The Bureau of Labor Statistics estimates of multifactor productivity growth are also shown in table 1-3. Between 1960 and 1973 multifactor productivity growth in the business sector as a whole was the same as in manufacturing, averaging 2 percent annually. By contrast, in the period 1973–89 manufacturing multifactor productivity growth was halved to 1.0 percent, and multifactor productivity growth in the business sector as a whole fell to just 0.5 percent. Indeed, given that manufacturing accounts for roughly a third of total business-sector output, this suggests there was virtually no increase in multifactor productivity growth outside manufacturing over this period.

Figure 1-2. *Alternative Measures for Relative Goods Prices, United States, 1959–79*[a]

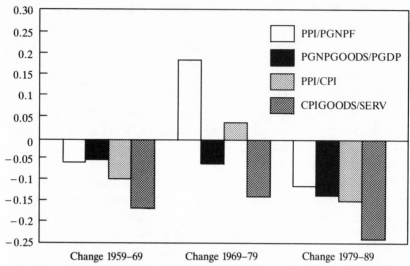

Change 1959–69   Change 1969–79   Change 1979–89

Sources: U.S. Department of Commerce and Bureau of Labor Statistics.
1st series, PPI/PGNPF = ratio of produce price index to GNP deflated fixed weight
2d series, PGNPGOODS/PGDP = ratio of GNP deflated for goods to GDP deflator
3d series, PPI/CPI = ratio of produce price index to consumer price index
4th series, CPI GOODS/SERV = ratio of consumer price index for goods to consumer price index for services

Some have suggested that this weak performance reflects problems that are inherent in improving productivity in services. But it is noteworthy that between 1950 and 1973 average annual growth in multifactor productivity in the private business sector was slightly higher than in manufacturing (3.0 percent versus 2.9 percent). Before 1973, therefore, there was nothing apparently inherent in nonmanufacturing that necessitated slower productivity growth.

Others believe that these data on nonmanufacturing productivity reflect considerable mismeasurement.[20] However, before 1973, measurement problems did not prevent the detection of significant productivity increases outside manufacturing. To attribute the entire slowdown in services productivity to measurement problems, one must argue not only that productivity in services is difficult to measure but that this measurement has recently grown more difficult.

Finally, still others have argued that trade has kept the U.S. manufacturing sector smaller than it would otherwise have been and has thus

20. See Baily and Gordon (1988) for a more extensive analysis.

reduced overall productivity growth. But the U.S. trade deficit in manufacturing in 1990 was just 6.5 percent of value-added in manufacturing. Had the manufacturing sector been 6.5 percent larger thanks to the elimination of the trade deficit, it would indeed have carried a larger weight in the business sector. But this larger weight would have increased the level of business-sector productivity growth accumulated between 1979 and 1990 by only 0.3 percent. Eliminating the trade deficit, therefore, would not have appreciably boosted American productivity.

In sum, over the 1980s the U.S. share of employment in manufacturing declined rapidly. About one-third of this decline reflects the impact of slow output growth, in part due to the growing trade deficit, and two-thirds, the relatively rapid rate of manufacturing productivity growth. But the impact of this deindustrialization on the growth in *average* economywide U.S. compensation and output per worker has been relatively small.

International Comparisons

Data on productivity and earnings in other countries in the Organization for Economic Cooperation and Development (OECD) are difficult to obtain. The BLS, however, does compile data on output and earnings per worker for France, Germany, Japan, and the United Kingdom. These data, expressed in national currencies, are reported in table 1-5. Several features are worth noting. First, in contrast to the U.S. experience, real earnings in the four economies grew significantly over the decade. The result has been a convergence of foreign real earnings toward U.S. levels.

Second, the primary source of the difference in earnings behavior between the United States and other countries was the difference in the growth of nonmanufacturing output per employee. Table 1-5 decomposes overall productivity growth between the manufacturing and nonmanufacturing sectors of each country. Almost all the U.S. productivity growth and a high share of the U.K. productivity growth occurred in manufacturing. In contrast, in Japan, France, and Germany productivity growth in nonmanufacturing contributed, respectively, 57 percent, 67 percent, and 75 percent to the total rise in productivity. These figures imply that productivity growth outside manufacturing (plus changes in the share of manufacturing in overall output) accounted for 70 percent, 91 percent, and more than 100 percent of the differences in overall productivity growth between the United States and Japan, France, and Germany,

Table 1-5. *Percent Changes in Real Earnings, United States and Four Other OECD Countries, 1979–89*[a]

Country	Comp /CPI (1)	Comp /POut (2)	Output per employee (3)	Change in output due to		
				Manufacturing (4)	Non-manufacturing (5)	Share change (6)
United States	2.1	5.4	7.6	6.4	2.2	−1.0
Japan	24.9	32.4	32.1	13.7	18.1	0.3
France	14.9	16.3	24.1	7.9	21.1	−4.9
Germany	11.3	9.4	13.8	3.5	12.3	−2.0
United Kingdom	14.0	12.1	17.1	13.2	4.6	−0.7
Difference from United States						
Japan	22.8	27.0	24.5	7.3	15.9	1.3
France	12.8	10.9	16.5	1.5	18.9	−3.9
Germany	9.2	4.0	6.2	−2.9	10.1	−1.0
United Kingdom	11.9	6.7	9.5	6.8	2.4	0.3

Supplementary information

Country	Output per employee		Manufacturing output per hour (9)	Labor share in income		Manufacturing real compensation	
	Manufacturing (7)	Other (8)		1979 (10)	1989	Annual (11)	Hourly
United States	30.7	2.8	27.3	60.2	59.0	3.1	0
Japan	52.2	24.5	30.3	54.2	54.3	19.6	19.7
France	33.8	27.5	42.3	54.9	51.7	13.2	20.3
Germany	10.5	18.5	18.9	57.0	54.8	18.3	27.1
United Kingdom	56.1	5.4	58.9	58.5	56.0	19.4	21.7

Sources: U.S. Bureau of Labor Statistics, Office of Productivity and Technology. releases on international productivity and GDP; OECD national income accounts.
a. Comp = average hourly compensation
CPI = consumer price index
POut = GDP deflator
(4) = (7)* 1979 share of manufacturing in output
(5) = (8)* 1979 share of nonmanufacturing in output
(6) = (3) − (4) − (5).

respectively. Differences between the United States and the United Kingdom, by contrast, reflected mainly manufacturing performance.

It is particularly striking that the United Kingdom and the United States stand out internationally in three respects. They both had rising inequality in blue-collar wages; they both experienced relatively rapid increases in manufacturing productivity; they both experienced substantial increases in the ratio of skilled to unskilled workers in manufacturing. In chapter 3, I show that these factors all made important contributions to the rising premium earned by educated workers in the United States.

Third, in the three European economies a shift in income distribution toward profits slowed down the growth in product wages, and production-wage and consumption-wage growth were similar. In these two respects the three economies differed from the United States. Japan, however, resembled the United States. There, profit shares remained constant, but consumption-wage growth lagged production-wage growth.

As noted in McKinsey, output per hour in the service sector remains higher in the United States than in other developed economies.[21] However, this American lead has been shrinking over the past two decades. Since most services are not traded, the improved relative performance abroad is likely to reflect domestic developments there—increased education, increased investment rates, and technological and organizational improvements—rather than the removal of barriers to trade.[22]

It is striking how much attention has focused on relative U.S. manufacturing performance and how little on the slowdown in U.S. services-productivity growth. Before the quantitative importance of this productivity development has been taken into account, it is particularly inappropriate to interpret the convergence in international real wages as evidence in support of factor-price equalization. FPE is a basic result of standard international trade theory which says that under certain conditions (including identical technology across countries, reasonably similar factor endowments across countries, and the absence of complete specialization), free trade equalizes factor prices across countries. It is important, therefore, to distinguish international factor-price convergence caused by FPE from international factor-price convergence caused by

21. McKinsey (1992).

22. Foreign direct investment, on the other hand, may have contributed to this convergence. According to the United Nations, in 1970 foreign direct investment in services accounted for 25 percent of the global stock of foreign direct investment. By the late 1980s the share was close to 50 percent. UNCTC (1991).

productivity or technological convergence. This distinction is critical because technological catch-up in the nontraded sector of follower nations might well *improve* rather than *reduce* real wages in the leading country.[23]

Conclusions

Trade has played a very small part in the performance of average real compensation in the United States. Consumption-deflated compensation has lagged production-deflated compensation because of the relative rise in housing prices and the relative decline in investment prices (especially computers). Compensation grew slowly mainly because service-sector productivity grew slowly. These results indicate that the most important determinants of U.S. average compensation lay in the behavior of the *domestic* economy.

The evidence shows that had American workers chosen to consume the products they produced, their real compensation would have increased by about 10 percent over the 1980s—about as much as output per worker in the business sector. However, real wage growth lagged productivity growth for two main reasons: first, much of the productivity growth occurred in industries producing capital goods such as computers, which workers do not generally buy; second, there were large increases in the relative price of housing (which workers consume but do not produce). International trade played no part in the poor average wage growth. Prices of U.S. exports rose slightly faster than the prices of the goods the United States imports; the resulting improvement in the terms of trade actually added to real consumption per worker in the United States.

The view that U.S. wages could enjoy a sustained increase if only workers were more powerful is fundamentally mistaken. The truth is that even with the most generous of employers, the plight of American workers would have been pretty much the same. If workers had received the same share of income in the corporate sector in 1995 as they received in 1979, taking account of inflation, their hourly compensation would have grown by a total of 7.2 percent. In other words, it would have been just 1.8 percent higher than it actually was. Qualitatively, therefore, the picture would have been essentially unchanged.

---

23. Much depends on the impact of foreign income growth on the terms of trade.

CHAPTER TWO

Wage Inequality:
Quantity Approaches

SINCE THE LATE 1970s the U.S. labor market has experienced growing inequality along the lines of skill, education, and occupation. As measured by the Employment Cost Index, between 1981 and 1991 the relative compensation of blue-collar workers compared with white-collar workers (outside of sales) declined by 12 percent. While there is evidence that in the 1990s the trend toward increased inequality has slowed or even ceased (see figure 2-1), the debate over the sources of inequality continues to rage.[1]

The process of wage determination is highly complex. Wages reflect a host of factors on both the demand and the supply sides of labor and product markets. In the 1980s, however, domestic supply-side factors alone do little to help explain the growing wage dispersion in the United States. In particular, the relative increase in the wages of educated workers and managers occurred even though the share of such workers in the labor force rose rapidly. Similarly, relative female wages rose despite the relatively rapid increase in female participation.[2] To explain the growing dispersion, therefore, most analysts have turned to demand-side expla-

---

1. Bound and Johnson (1995).
2. Supply-side stories that emphasize changes in growth rates may do better. Although the relative supply of educated labor increased in the 1980s, it grew more slowly than in the 1970s. Thus in the face of a given increase in the relative demand for skilled labor, wages of skilled workers would rise. For an argument along these lines, see Katz and Murphy (1992).

Figure 2-1. *U.S. Blue- and White-Collar Compensation, 1981–95*

1981 = 100

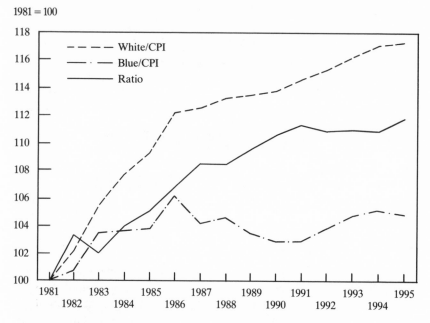

Source: Employment Cost Index.

nations such as trade and technology. For example, Robert Reich has argued that global competition has bifurcated American workers—and thereby American society—into two groups: high-earning "symbolic analysts," whose talents are rewarded by globalization, and the mass of ordinary production workers, whose earnings are depressed by it.[3] Likewise, many others have argued that international trade has played an important role.[4]

The empirical evidence in support of this view, however, remains a matter of contention. Several researchers have found correlations between the emergence of trade deficits and rising wage inequality. Some of this evidence has come from time-series studies of the United States. In particular Kevin Murphy and Finis Welch found a correspondence between the patterns of wage growth and durable goods performance and conclude that "the evolving pattern of international trade is perhaps a primary cause of recent wage changes."[5] Similarly, George Borjas and

3. Reich (1991).

4. See, for example, Leamer (1992); Wood (1994); Sachs and Shatz (1994).

5. Murphy and Welch (1991, p. 43).

Valerie Ramey report a strong association between trade deficits in durable goods and wage inequality between 1963 and 1988 (although it has broken down more recently).[6] Other evidence has come from cross-sectional international studies. Adrian Wood finds that countries with the largest increases in wage inequality over the past two decades have the largest increases in trade deficits with developing countries.[7] He argues that the growth of manufacturing exports from newly developing countries explains not only the rise in earnings inequality but also the trend toward higher unemployment in both Europe and North America.

But these findings of correlations between trade and wage behavior, while suggestive, do not establish causation. It would help our understanding if the structural linkages between trade and wages could be modeled and used to test whether the quantitative effects of such findings are plausible.

Net Factor Content

Some studies have gauged the quantitative impact of trade by using estimates of the net factor content of trade. This approach treats imports as increasing the supply of productive factors and exports as increasing the demand for those factors. Typically, such studies use input-output methods to estimate the different types of labor used in the production of traded goods. For example, Borjas, Richard Freeman, and Lawrence Katz estimate the quantities of educated and uneducated labor embodied in U.S. manufactured exports and imports.[8] Since U.S. imports contain relatively more uneducated labor, an increase in net imports raises the relative supply of uneducated labor and drives down its relative wage. Their quantitative estimates, however, suggest the impact is fairly small. They conclude that trade flows explained at most 15 percent (that is, 1.9 percentage points) of the 12.4 percent increase between 1980 and 1988 in the earnings differential between college-educated workers and their high-school-educated counterparts.

Similarly, Jeffrey Sachs and Howard Shatz estimate a counterfactual scenario in which U.S. net trade balances remained a constant share of final demand between 1978 and 1990. Using an input-output analysis,

6. Borjas and Ramey (1994).
7. Wood (1994).
8. Borjas, Freeman, and Katz (1992, p. 237).

they conclude that trade reduced U.S. manufacturing employment by 5.9 percent between 1978 and 1990, a number equal to about 1 percent of total U.S. employment. They also provide separate estimates of the impact of trade on the demand for production and nonproduction workers. They conclude that all manufactured trade resulted in declines in production and nonproduction workers of 7.2 percent and 2.1 percent, respectively, the bulk of this decline being attributable to trade with developing countries, which reduced manufacturing employment by 5.7 percent and production and nonproduction employment by 6.2 percent and 4.3 percent, respectively.[9]

In table 2-1, I build on the work of Sachs and Shatz to estimate the impact of trade on the net demand for workers with different levels of education. In their counterfactual scenario, Sachs and Shatz report the impact of trade on nineteen two-digit U.S. manufacturing industries. I have used estimates of employment by education level in these industries drawn from Current Population Survey data.[10] Applying these estimates suggests that between 1978 and 1990 trade reduced the employment of workers in U.S. manufacturing with a high-school education or less by 6.8 percent and workers with a college degree by 4.7 percent. Again, the bulk of the effect is due to trade with developing countries. But since in 1990 high-school workers in manufacturing accounted for only about a quarter of high-school workers in the U.S. economy as a whole, the impact of these effects on the overall relative demand for such workers was small.

When one considers with whom America trades and the scale of U.S. trade, it is not surprising that estimates of the factor supplies embodied in U.S. manufacturing trade show relatively small effects on wages, particularly for trade with developing countries. In 1990, 70 percent of America's manufacturing imports came from OECD countries, countries with endowments and wage levels similar to America's.[11] U.S. imports from developing countries did increase rapidly over the decade but from a low base. In 1990, for example, imports of manufactured goods (classified on an international trade basis) amounted to 2.1 percent of U.S. GNP, as opposed to 1.2 percent in 1981.[12] A change of this magnitude—less than

9. Sachs and Shatz (1994, p. 29).
10. These data were generously provided by Howard Shatz and Jeffrey Sachs.
11. In 1980 hourly compensation in other OECD countries was 83 percent of U.S. levels; this dropped to 64 percent by 1985 but then increased to 103 percent by 1990.
12. Imports of manufactured goods into the European Community in 1988–89

Table 2-1. *U.S. Manufacturing Employment and the Impact of Trade, 1978 and 1990*
Employment in thousands, unless otherwise specified

Item	High school[a]	College[b]	Production	Nonproduction	Total manufacturing	Total U.S. employment[c]
1978	13,780.38	5,458.22	14,227.90	5,010.70	19,238.60	90,406.00
1990	10,839.44	6,718.46	12,111.80	5,446.10	17,557.90	109,419.00
Percent change	−21.34	23.09	−14.87	8.69	−8.74	21.03
1990 (no trade)	11,778.57	6,973.58	13,093.15	5,659.01	⋯	⋯
Percent change	−14.53	27.78	−7.98	12.94	⋯	⋯
Trade impact	−6.82	−4.67	−6.90	−4.25	⋯	⋯

Sources: National Bureau of Economic Research productivity data set; NBER Current Population Survey merged data files. 1978 high-school and college workers estimated using 1979 ratios; trade impact estimated using Sachs and Shatz (1994) counterfactual scenario.
a. High school = workers with high-school education or less.
b. College = workers with some college education.
c. Millions.

Table 2-2. *U.S. Manufacturing Trade with Developing Countries,*
1978 and 1990

Standard industrial classification	Ratio of trade balance to value added		Percent change	1990 ratio of imports to value added
	1978	1990		
20 Food	0.044	−0.005	−0.049	0.053
21 Tobacco	0.081	0.061	−0.020	0.002
22 Textiles	−0.007	−0.108	−0.101	0.164
23 Apparel	−0.020	−0.629	−0.609	0.680
24 Lumber	0.013	−0.007	−0.020	0.061
25 Furniture	−0.012	−0.100	−0.087	0.123
26 Paper	−0.013	0.040	0.053	0.018
27 Printing	−0.000	−0.001	−0.001	0.006
28 Chemicals	0.072	0.077	0.006	0.023
29 Petroleum	0.014	−0.157	−0.171	0.285
30 Rubber	0.027	−0.055	−0.081	0.093
31 Leather	0.040	−1.864	−1.905	2.011
32 Stone, glass	0.019	−0.030	−0.049	0.064
33 Primary metals	0.021	−0.082	−0.103	0.164
34 Fabricated metals	0.030	−0.008	−0.038	0.055
35 Nonelectrical machinery	0.126	0.040	−0.085	0.116
36 Electric machinery	0.090	−0.059	−0.149	0.199
37 Transportation	0.073	0.072	−0.001	0.058
38 Instruments	0.065	0.032	−0.033	0.063
39 Miscellaneous manufacturing	0.042	−0.529	−0.570	0.599
Total Manufacturing	0.050	−0.026	−0.076	0.112

Source: OECD STAN Database.

1 percent of GNP—is unlikely to have an overwhelming effect on the whole labor market.

Between 1978 and 1990 the U.S. trade balance in manufactured goods with developing countries shifted from a surplus of $32.8 billion to a deficit of $34.9 billion. In 1978 the surplus with developing countries in manufactured goods was equal to 5 percent of total value-added in U.S. manufacturing; in 1990 the deficit was equal to 2.6 percent (table 2-2). Overall, therefore, the shift was equal to 7.6 percent of value-added in manufacturing. Since manufactured products embody primary commodities and services not produced in manufacturing, this ratio exaggerates

amounted to $89 billion, or less than 2 percent of GNP. On a standard industrial classification (SIC) basis, in which petroleum and food imports are classified as manufacturing, U.S. imports from developing countries were $148.2 billion in 1990.

the negative effect of the manufacturing trade deficit on manufacturing value-added and employment.

Though small in the aggregate, it should be noted that the impact of trade is not insubstantial for certain sectors. In particular, imports from developing countries are concentrated in a few major industries: apparel (15 percent), electrical goods (18.4 percent), so-called nonelectrical machinery, which includes computers (10.4 percent), miscellaneous manufacturing (8 percent), and leather (6.2 percent) account for well over half of all imports. As shown in table 2-2, in some of these sectors the effects on total value-added were very important.

As for other OECD countries, their trade volumes and trade balances in manufactured goods with developing countries are small compared with the size of their economies. Although it has been growing rapidly, the share of imports from developing countries remains a very small share of the overall consumption of manufactured goods and in the GDP of OECD economies (table 2-3). According to Pierre-André Buiges and Alexis Jacquemin, European Community (EU) imports of manufactured goods from developing countries increased by 1.9 percent of total demand between 1982 and 1992. But in 1992 they still represented only 5.2 percent of total demand for manufactured goods; that is, output − exports + imports. In that year the ratios were lowest in France (3.8 percent) and Italy (4.3 percent), and though higher in the United Kingdom (5.2 percent) and Germany (5.6 percent), they still were small compared with the overall market. At the same time, 7.2 percent of EU manufactured output was exported to the developing nations, with shares of 6.1 percent for the United Kingdom, 7 percent for Germany, and 7.5 percent each for France and Italy.[13] With trade flows of these orders of magnitude, developing countries are unlikely to have large effects on the labor market by operating through the channel of net factor content.[14]

The factor-content approach provides a sense of the orders of magnitude of the impact of trade on employment when wages and prices are relatively rigid. Applications of this approach to major OECD economies besides the United States also show that the effects of trade with devel-

13. Buiges and Jacquemin (1994, pp. 7–9).
14. Imports into Europe from low-wage countries are heavily concentrated in the same sectors as in the United States. According to Buiges and Jacquemin, in 1992 they accounted for 80.7 percent of overall demand in "other manufacturing industries" (toys, jewelry, musical instruments), 29.0 percent in leather, 25.8 percent in footwear and clothing, 15 percent in textiles, and 12.8 percent in office and computing machinery.

Table 2-3. *Imports of Manufactures to OECD Regions or Countries from Non-OECD Regions, Selected Years, 1962–93*

Billions of dollars

Region or country and year	Latin America	Central Europe and former USSR	Africa	Middle East	Asia	Total	Ratio of total to GDP
North America							
1963	0.2	0	0.1	0.1	0.5	0.9	n.a.
1973	2.0	0.3	0.3	0.3	5.6	8.5	n.a.
1980	7.0	1.1	2.5	1.0	23.9	35.5	n.a.
1993	46.8	2.3	1.8	5.1	139.7	195.7	0.028
Western Europe							
1963	0.1	0.9	0.2	0.2	0.6	2.0	n.a.
1973	1.1	4.2	0.9	0.7	4.0	10.9	n.a.
1980	3.4	13.5	5.1	3.3	20.5	45.8	n.a.
1992	8.6	26.9	12.4	7.4	95.7	15.1	0.021
Japan							
1963	0	0	0	0	0.1	0.1	n.a.
1973	0	0.1	0.1	0.2	2.3	2.7	n.a.
1980	0.5	0.3	0.3	0.2	5.8	7.1	n.a.
1993	1.2	0.6	0.4	1.1	44.7	48.0	n.a.
Total							
1963	0.3	1.0	0.3	0.2	1.3	3.1	n.a.
1973	3.1	4.7	1.3	1.2	11.9	22.2	n.a.
1980	10.9	14.9	7.9	4.5	50.2	88.4	n.a.
1992	50.4	28.8	14.1	12.7	257.8	363.8	n.a.

	Share of GDP in total trade with non-OECD				
Country and year	Imports (1)	OPEC (2)	Non-OPEC (3)	Exports (4)	Net exports (4 − 3)
United States					
1962	1.02	0.26	0.76	1.55	0.79
1972	1.12	0.22	0.9	1.18	0.28
1982	2.83	0.99	1.84	2.56	0.72
1993	3.23	0.53	2.7	2.42	− 0.28
Europe					
1962	4.38	1.19	3.19	3.61	0.42
1972	3.94	1.37	2.57	3.43	0.86
1982	6.64	2.86	3.78	5.94	2.16
1992	3.96	0.76	3.2	3.8	0.6
Japan					
1962	3.88	1.12	2.76	3.94	1.18
1972	3.72	1.5	2.22	5.23	3.01
1982	7.67	4.45	3.22	6.22	3.0
1993	2.96	0.89	2.07	4.52	2.45

Source: GATT International Trade, 1994.
n.a. Not available.
a. OPEC = Organization of Petroleum Exporting Countries.

Table 2-4. *Sources of Declining Share of Manufacturing Employment in Five OECD Countries, OECD Estimates, Selected Periods, 1968–86*
Percent unless otherwise specified

Country and period	Change in share	Due to trade All	Due to trade Non-OECD	Due to productivity	Due to output expansion
United States, 1972–85	−5.00	−1.10	−0.76	−5.96	0.96
United Kingdom, 1968–84	−12.34	−2.89	−0.38	−14.74	2.40
Japan, 1970–85	−2.48	8.86	2.47	−20.69	18.21
Germany, 1978–86	−2.14	1.41	−1.00	−3.62	1.48
France, 1972–85	−4.4	1.55	0.97	−9.12	4.72

| | Change in employment in manufacturing (thousands) | | | | |
| | | Due to trade | | | |
Country and period	Total	All	Non-OECD	Due to productivity	Due to output expansion
United States, 1972–85	305	−458	−540	−5,710	6,015
United Kingdom, 1968–84	−3,249	−784	−120	−3,597	348
Japan, 1970–85	251	5,640	1,616	−12,261	12,512
Germany, 1978–86	−326	477	−240	−961	635
France, 1972–85	−917	339	210	−1,948	1,031
Total	−1,732	2,204	926	−3,936	20,541

Source: Sakurai (1993).

oping countries are small. Norihisa Sakurai has undertaken a sophisticated input-output analysis that decomposes employment changes into several sources.[15] Although the analysis ends in the mid-1980s, it is extremely illuminating. On balance, over the periods for which data are available, generally from the early 1970s to the mid-1980s, trade with developing countries boosted manufacturing employment in the aggregate in five major industrial countries (table 2-4). However, while the effects on France were positive, most of the increase occurred in Japan. In the United States, the United Kingdom, and Germany, manufactured trade with non-OECD countries depressed manufacturing employment by 540,000, 120,000, and 240,000, respectively. Again, these are not surprising results. Although the external manufacturing trade of the OECD as a whole has grown fairly rapidly, it still remains small relative to overall manufacturing value-added and relative to the economy as a whole.

In 1992 in the United Kingdom and former West Germany, unemployment stood at 2.7 million and 1.8 million, respectively. Assuming, for

15. Sakurai (1995, p. 154).

example, that all workers displaced because of this trade with developing countries were added to the unemployment roles in the United Kingdom and Germany, they would account for 4.4 percent and 13.2 percent of the total unemployment, respectively. Moreover, these shifts took place over a decade or more. This suggests that even under the assumption that wages and prices domestically are fixed, manufactured trade with developing countries probably had little effect on aggregate unemployment levels in these economies. Thus though undoubtedly more important in relatively labor-intensive sectors, the magnitudes of the trade involved preclude the net-factor-content approach from finding huge effects on the labor market.[16]

Challenges

The applications of the factor-content approach to derive labor-market effects of trade has been heavily criticized by some trade economists. In particular, Jagdish Bhagwati and Edward Leamer, among others, have emphasized that relative price changes are a critical intervening variable in the chain of causation from trade to factor prices and have argued against using factor content to estimate the impact of trade on wages.[17] However, the major problem does not really rest on whether price or quantity evidence is examined. Instead, applying the net-factor-content approach empirically to explain historical episodes requires assuming that the trade flows actually observed were caused only by the change in the trading opportunities available to the country and not by other changes, such as technology, tastes, and relative factor supplies. In practice this assumption will not hold, and it is not easy to identify these effects separately because they are interactive. Changes in demand, factor supplies, technology, and opportunities to trade internationally could all affect the composition of trade, output, and relative product and factor prices. In particular, as Deardorff and Hakura have emphasized, the volume of trade is an endogenous variable that is simultaneously determined with wages. If trade is generated by a decline in trade barriers at home or abroad, the impacts on wages could be very different than if

16. In a framework with fixed prices and wages, trade changes could give rise to multiplier effects, reducing output by more than the initial trade change. See Krugman (1995b). Nonetheless, even doubling or trebling these effects suggests they remain small.

17. Bhagwati (1991); Leamer (forthcoming).

trade is generated by changes in tastes or technology.[18] Nonetheless, provided the only source of trade is changes in trade opportunities, as Paul Krugman and Alan Deardorff and Robert Staiger have demonstrated, there will be a relationship between the factor content of trade and relative factor prices.[19] Indeed, under certain conditions (namely, that both production and consumption functions have unitary elasticities of substitution, that is, are Cobb-Douglas) changes in relative factor prices will be proportional to the total changes in relative factor supplies represented by trade flows.[20]

Adrian Wood contends that the traditional studies are flawed because they use factor-content measures derived from developed-country production data. This implicitly assumes that imports and domestic products are similar. Wood argues, on the contrary, that imports from developing countries are actually noncompeting trade. He believes that trade with developing countries has eliminated the most labor-intensive products from developed-country production. This means developed-country imports of these products are far more labor intensive than suggested by the conventional net-factor-content methodologies.[21]

Wood's approach yields much larger estimates of the impact of developing-country trade on employment in the North. His work is thus a fundamental challenge to the studies, cited above, which conclude that

18. Deardorff and Hakura (1994). Leamer (1996) emphasizes that the net-factor-content approach can (only) be used to compare two equilibriums that have the same tastes, technologies, and factor supplies and that differ only in terms of external trading opportunities.

19. Krugman (1995b); Deardorff and Staiger (1988).

20. Deardorff and Staiger demonstrate that under conditions of incomplete specialization each trading equilibrium is associated with an equivalent autarky equilibrium. If the factors embodied in the country's exports are subtracted from its initial endowment, and those embodied in imports are added to its initial supply, then with the same prices of goods as prevailed in the trading equilibrium a competitive autarkic equilibrium exists in which the consumption of goods and factor prices are the same as in the trading equilibrium. The key idea is that the country is given through trade the very endowment equal to the factor content of equilibrium consumption. Thus the country can produce what it consumes and not have to trade. Robert Baldwin and Glen Cain (1994, p. 32). have drawn on this methodology to analyze U.S. manufacturing trade over the period 1977–87 under the assumption of unitary elasticities. They estimate that trade accounted for 2.3 percentage points of the 17 percentage point increase in the earnings gap between workers with more than twelve years of education and workers with twelve years or less. (Without trade the gap would have been 50 percent if factor trade had been the same as in 1977, whereas it was actually 52.3 percent.) These results are similar to those of Borjas, Freeman, and Katz.

21. Wood (1994, p. 149).

trade with the South, though important for sectors such as clothing, footwear, and electronics, has not been a major factor in overall labor-market performance. In his preferred base-case scenario Wood concludes that manufactured-goods trade with the South reduced employment in northern manufacturing by 9.0 million person years, the equivalent of 12.1 percent of manufacturing employment in the North in the base year. In this scenario the effects on relative factor demands are also large. Trade increases the economywide demand for skilled workers by 0.1 percent but reduces economywide demand for unskilled workers by 5.3 percent. By contrast, Wood shows that had he applied the conventional net-factor-content method to his data, he would have concluded that trade between the North and the South reduced northern manufacturing employment by just 1.1 million, about 1.5 percent of manufacturing employment.[22]

In these alternative calculations, Wood sets up a model that is a special case of the two-goods Heckscher-Ohlin (HO) model, in which technological capabilities are assumed to be similar worldwide.[23] Under conditions of autarky, both the North and the South produce developed-country and developing-country goods. With trade, each is driven to a corner solution and specializes in the production of only one good. In the traditional two-goods HO model, nations continue to produce both goods—production remains within the zone of diversification—and there is a unique link between the prices of goods and factors of production. In this standard case, with factor prices equalized, it does not matter that factor-content estimates are obtained from developed-country data, since the same goods are produced everywhere with similar input-output co-efficients. Given complete specialization, however, the link between relative-traded goods prices and relative factor prices breaks down.

Since, according to Wood, developing-country goods are no longer produced in the North, Wood is faced with the task of estimating the factor inputs that would be used to produce these goods in the North. He does this by assuming that technology is the same worldwide and using input-output coefficients from southern data. However, Wood observes that factor prices are not equalized worldwide and therefore adjusts these coefficients to reflect the fact that when produced in the North, developing-country goods will embody relatively more skilled labor. In

22. Wood (1994, p. 149).
23. Wood (1994, p. 149).

addition, since develoing-country goods produced in the North will be more expensive, Wood makes adjustments to reflect shifts in demand.

Wood has made a valuable contribution to the debate. He is certainly correct to point out that the conventional net-factor-content studies have a downward bias, and that the goods displaced by developing countries are likely to be more labor intensive than those produced on average in any given industry. Accordingly, the more aggregated the input-output table used, the more likely the understatement of the labor content of developing country trade. However, Wood's alternative approach has several problems of its own. In what follows, I first describe that approach and then indicate why his results are problematic.

Similar technologies. Wood's approach rests critically on the assumption that technology is similar worldwide. If in reality the North's technology is superior, the procedure will be wrong. Unfortunately for Wood, his results suggest that the assumption of similar technologies is invalid. In particular, Wood estimates that if developed-country goods were produced in the South, their prices would be 50 percent lower than in the North! It strains credulity to believe that the South could produce at half the price the high-tech jet aircraft and computers they import from the North. Moreover, this implies his model has a serious problem: why do developing countries import something they could produce far more cheaply at home?

Wood himself remarks that his estimate of the costs of producing developed-country goods in developing countries is "not believable." And because of these problems he estimates the impact of trade on the South with an arbitrary correction factor. Wood does offer an explanation for the result. He suggests that it may indicate a failure to allow for the fact that "skilled workers are more productive when clustered together."[24] But if such clusters are important, workers in the North could also be more productive when producing developing-country goods, and the assumption of similar technological capabilities would then be inappropriate. Indeed, if clusters (or other externalities of scale) made the North more productive than the South, trade with the South would lead to much smaller job loss than Wood projects.

Elasticity parameters. The parameters Wood uses are outliers rather than reasonable central estimates. He estimates that relative factor prices are dramatically different worldwide. Taking account of differences in

24. Wood (1994, p. 137).

labor quality, the price of unskilled labor (compared with skilled labor) in the North is three times as high as in the South. To estimate the inputs used in the North to produce developing-country goods, one needs to adjust the input coefficients derived from southern production data to reflect factor prices. Wood makes this adjustment using an assumed parameter for the elasticity of substitution between factors. In addition, in the absence of trade the relative prices of goods would shift. Wood estimates that if the developing-country goods were to be produced in the North, their cost would be almost 2.8 times higher.[25]

Two parameters therefore play a crucial role in Wood's counterfactual calculations. The elasticity of substitution between skilled and unskilled labor and the elasticity of demand between developed-country and developing-country goods. Since unskilled workers are more expensive in the North, a high elasticity of substitution means fewer employment opportunities for unskilled workers in the counterfactual scenario. Similarly, since developing-country goods are more expensive when produced in the North, a high elasticity of demand implies fewer sales and thus fewer employment opportunities for unskilled workers. The higher these elasticities, therefore, the smaller is the impact of southern imports on the demand for unskilled labour in the North.

Wood also provides the reader with estimates of the impact of alternative assumptions. He claims that doing so indicates the robustness of his results. But, in fact, he demonstrates that his results are very sensitive to the specific parameters used and that reasonable parameters would fundamentally change his conclusions. In his base case, in which the price elasticity of demand is set at 0.5, without trade the relative demand for uneducated labor in the North increases by 9.0 million person years. However, if the assumed price elasticity is raised from 0.5 to 0.8, the impact falls from 9.0 million to 6.4 million person years. Similarly, if the substitution elasticity is raised from 0.5 to 0.9, the impact of trade falls from 9.0 million to 6.3 million. Wood is aware of the importance of these parameters and notes that assuming an elasticity of substitution of 2.0 (and 0.5 for demand) leads to results where there are no adverse effects on unskilled labor at all.[26]

What are reasonable estimates of these elasticities? Wood severely biases his results by choosing estimates that are very low. He notes that

25. Wood (1994, p. 137).
26. Wood (1994, p. 736).

"most estimates of the elasticity of substitution between highly educated and less educated are between 1.0 and 2.0."[27] But he dismisses these as upwardly biased because, he argues, such estimates usually capture not simply the pure elasticity of substitution but also the changes in quality and product mix induced by such wage changes. In other words, when the price of a factor falls, this not only leads to the factor's increased use in making a given quantity of goods but also shifts the product mix toward other goods and qualities that use the factor relatively intensively.

But how large is this bias? By marking down the elasticity estimates of between unity and 2.0 in the literature to 0.5, Wood is implicitly assuming that these effects are twice as large as the pure substitution effect—which is surely a huge exaggeration, particularly since there is no evidence on which to base this adjustment. Wood does cite some case studies that find much smaller substitution possibilities, but he himself notes that these "are biased downwards."[28] Thus even accepting Wood's critique of the existing studies, one could disagree with his choice of 0.5 as the central parameter in his analysis. An estimate of unity would actually be conservative, given the wide range found in the literature.[29]

Even more questionable is Wood's choice of demand elasticities. To rationalize his parameter choice, Wood quotes studies that have estimated demand elasticities for *entire* categories of goods for small price changes. In particular, Wood cites estimates of elasticities of demand for clothing and footwear of between 0.5 and 0.8. These are naturally low. But the estimates do not refer to the demand for the products now made in the South but instead relate to total demand for such goods. The overall demand for toys may be 0.5, for example, but this would not mean that the demand elasticity for developing-country dolls relative to developed-country dolls should be taken as 0.5. In fact, Gene Grossman explicitly estimated the substitutability of goods imported from developing countries and those produced in the United States and found, in contrast to Wood's assertions, that "imports from . . . LDCs are in most

27. Wood (1994, p. 132).
28. Wood (1994, p. 133).
29. It is important to distinguish two uses for the elasticity of substitution parameter. One, in the context of Wood's model, is to estimate what the actual use was historically to produce a specific good. In this context, Wood is correct in seeking an estimate capturing a narrow notion. However, for more general purposes of estimating the impact of a change in relative-factor supplies, we would want the broader notion that takes account of the modifications of product varieties and qualities and technological change to which changed supplies give rise.

cases relatively close substitutes for domestically produced commodities." Among the eleven categories Grossman estimated, only in three (all various types of steel products) did he obtain estimates lower than 0.5. Indeed, in six categories elasticities were greater than unity, ranging as high as 2.0 for cameras, 2.6 for typewriters, and 8.0 for television receivers.[30]

Moreover, one should keep in mind that most demand and substitution elasticities are estimated for fairly small price changes. Many of the standardized, lower-quality products currently made only in the South are actually substitutes for more expensive products made in the North. The price changes Wood is simulating are very large, on the order of 300 percent. Today, for example, black-and-white TVs are made in the South, while many large color TVs are produced in the North. At three times the price, black-and-white TVs would be more expensive than many color models. Would any be sold at all? For the large price changes Wood is simulating, elasticities would surely be much larger than 0.5.

Finally, the key feature of developing-country products is that they are relatively standardized and concentrated in competitive markets. They compete on price rather than on quality or uniqueness. Indeed, Joaquim Oliveira-Martins finds that to be true for OECD imports from East Asia. These are precisely the kinds of products for which demand is likely to collapse in the presence of threefold increases in price. Moreover, the fact that many are used as inputs may mean that in the short run demand is less elastic, but over the longer periods of time relevant here, that would not be true. Again, to use demand elasticity parameters of unity twice the size of Wood's would still be reasonably conservative.

Services and technology. Wood further argues that his estimates for manufacturing trade underestimate the full impact of trade between the North and the South for two reasons. First, they are confined to manufacturing trade and ignore both trade in services and the indirect effects of such trade on nontraded sectors that supply intermediate inputs to manufactured trade in services. Wood suggests that taking account of these effects would double those obtained for manufacturing alone. Since the value of trade in services is about half that in manufactured goods, Wood proposes increasing the estimated impact on factor demand by a half. In addition, he suggests that the inclusion of nontraded services would add another impact equal to about 40 percent.[31]

30. Grossman (1982, p. 277).
31. Wood (1994, p. 165).

Second, his estimates ignore the impact of trade in stimulating technical progress, which is biased against unskilled labor. Contending that this effect is "at least as important as the relocation and reallocation effects that are captured by the modified factor content method," he proposes doubling the earlier estimates.[32] All told, therefore, Wood argues that the economywide relative demand for unskilled labor has been reduced by 22 percent. Thus he concludes that although trade with the South has large aggregate benefits for the North, it leads to "rising inequality and mass unemployment."[33]

As I discuss in the next chapter, it is by no means clear that one would expect trade with developing countries to induce skill-biased technological change. Moreover, even if the effects Wood has identified may be relevant, his quantitative estimates are speculative and not based on hard evidence.[34] The issue of the magnitude of induced technical change, for example, is an important one, but why should one believe it is twice as large as the impact of the modified factor-content method? Why not six times as large or half as small? These magnification efforts are not credible and could provide misleading support for those, unlike Wood himself, who would like to use his work for protectionist purposes.

Conclusion

In summary, the net-factor-content approach suggests a role for trade in reducing employment opportunities and lowering the relative wages of unskilled workers in the OECD, but the effects have been relatively

32. Wood (1994, p. 167).

33. Wood (1994, p. 1). Wood's argument about induced technological change has more weight, of course, if imported goods are fairly close substitutes for domestic goods. It is less relevant if they are poor substitutes. Indeed, entrepreneurs in the North have little to fear from lower prices of noncompeting goods. The more relevant Wood's critique of conventional factor-content approaches becomes, therefore, the less relevant is his point about technological change.

34. In an appendix, Wood offers an analysis in which the greater shift in the ratio of skilled to unskilled workers in manufacturing than in the rest of the economy is ascribed to trade with developing countries. However, he actually finds that when education is used as a measure, "the increases in relative skill intensity are mainly rather small" (p. 409). He finds a tendency toward relatively faster manufacturing shifts in skill intensity as measured by professional and technical occupations but observes that such shifts were present in the 1960s before trade with developing countries was important. In reality, the shift toward white-collar occupations is more rapid in services. Wood summarizes his own results as inconclusive (p. 423).

small. A median view would be that they explain only about 10 percent of the rising differential between high-school and college workers in the United States, with a range of 10 percentage points encompassing most studies. This view has been challenged by some theorists who argue it rests on a shaky conceptual framework. In some cases the factor content of trade could be misleading; in particular, the factor content of the net trade balance could give the wrong result. But in fact, as Deardorff and Staiger and Krugman have shown, the net factor content of trade can be used to estimate the change in relative factor prices that could result from trade under the assumption of incomplete specialization, provided all changes in trade result from changing opportunities for trade and not from shfts in tastes or technology.[35] The traditional use of the net-factor-content approach has also been challenged by Wood on the ground that complete specialization has occurred. Wood is correct to point out that conventional factor-content approaches understate the labor content of trade with developing countries. But the effect is probably smaller than he suggests and his model is flawed by assuming similar technologies worldwide and by the use of very low elasticity parameters. Indeed, with parameters that are plausible, Wood's model would yield estimates that are much more similar to those obtained by conventional studies.

35. Deardorff and Staiger (1988); Krugman (1995a).

CHAPTER THREE

Wage Inequality: Price Evidence and Technological Change

THE STANDARD WORKHORSE of trade theorists, the Hecksher-Ohlin-Samuelson (HOS) model, assumes a world of constant returns to scale and perfect competition.[1] A basic implication of this model, typically set in a two-goods world with trade, is the Stolper-Samuelson theorem.[2] This theorem states that a rise in the price of a product raises the real return to factors used relatively intensively in the production of that good and lowers the real return to factors used relatively sparsely in the production of that good.

The Stolper-Samuelson theorem is in principle highly relevant for the shifts in relative factor prices that have been observed in the United States and elsewhere. The relative returns to less-educated workers in the United States have fallen, regardless of whether they are employed in industries that compete against developing countries. The attractive feature of the theorem is that it explains economywide factor returns on the basis of trade. Regardless of where they are employed, all owners of a given factor will experience similar changes in their factor returns.

---

1. This section draws heavily from Lawrence and Slaughter (1993).
2. See appendix 3A for a description of the Stolper-Samuelson process. See also Stolper and Samuelson (1941).

The model in which the Stolper-Samuelson theorem holds is very powerful because it establishes a tight connection between relative factor prices and the prices of internationally traded goods, provided that as many traded goods are produced domestically as there are factors of production. This link occurs, regardless of how small the volume of traded goods production and how large the nontraded sector. It means that changes in domestic relative-factor supplies or in the trade balance leave relative-factor prices unaffected unless they can affect the prices of internationally traded goods.[3]

If trade lowered the relative wages of unskilled workers, according to the Stolper-Samuelson theorem, one would expect to see a decline in the relative price of goods that are produced using unskilled labor relatively intensively. Consider, for example, the impact one would expect as large, labor-intensive economies such as China and India lowered their own trade barriers and entered the world market. In the first place, their presence would be felt through an increase in the global relative supply of unskilled-labor-intensive products. That, in turn, would lower the relative price of these products on world markets, thereby putting downward pressure on the wages of unskilled workers throughout the world.[4]

As I emphasized in the previous chapter when discussing the net-factor-content approach, trying to draw causal inferences by simply looking at historical data requires making some fairly strong assumptions about the nature of the shocks affecting the system. Traded-goods prices, like traded quantities, are endogenous variables that are affected by a wide number of shocks, of which an increase in the supply of goods coming from labor-intensive countries is just one.

Nonetheless, in Lawrence and Slaughter, Matthew Slaughter and I tried to see whether the traditional Stolper-Samuelson story fitted the facts for the U.S. economy in the 1980s. We therefore explored the behavior of U.S. prices over the 1980s.[5]

We used three-digit SIC-level employment and price data from U.S. manufacturing industries and had data for import prices, export prices, and domestic prices (that is, shipments deflators). We used occupational

3. For a discussion of models with complete specialization see appendix 3B.

4. In general, of course, besides price changes, one would also expect to see responses in trade volumes. The OECD would increase its imports of unskilled-labor-intensive products and its exports of skilled-labor-intensive products. Thus the net-factor-content approach considered in chapter 2 would provide some information, but a complementary inquiry would consider the price evidence directly.

5. Lawrence and Slaughter (1993).

categories to define two factors: production workers were assumed to be "unskilled" labor and nonproduction workers to be skilled labor. In a regression analysis we did not find statistically significant relationships between relative price changes and relative factor intensity. Similarly, we found that over the 1980s the relative import and export prices of unskilled-labor-intensive goods *increased* slightly. It is important to emphasize that we know from the Stolper-Samuelson theorem that the change in relative-factor prices will be larger than the change in relative-product prices—the so-called magnification effect. If exports and imports have fairly similar factor intensities, this impact could be large. It is therefore not surprising that large relative-price changes are difficult to detect in the data.

We also noted another feature of the U.S. labor market that was inconsistent with the simple Stolper-Samuelson story. In the pure Stolper-Samuelson case, either there is no within-industry shift in factor input ratios if coefficients are fixed, or there is a *downward* movement within industries in the ratio of skilled to unskilled workers if factor substitution is possible. In particular, if trade lowers the relative wages of unskilled workers, and, as is usually the case, it is possible to substitute between factors, the within-industry shifts will be toward using unskilled labor relatively more intensively. In Lawrence and Slaughter we found, however, that throughout U.S. manufacturing, in the 1980s, there was a pervasive *upward* shift within industries in the ratio of skilled to unskilled labor. Our conclusion, therefore, was that the simple Stolper-Samuelson process due to trade does not provide an adequate account of the growing wage inequality. Instead, we interpreted the evidence as consistent with a widespread bias in manufacturing technology toward the more intensive use of skilled labor and argued that skilled wages had also been raised by relatively rapid neutral productivity growth in technology-intensive sectors.

Eli Berman, John Bound, and Zvi Griliches reach a similar conclusion and demonstrate that the rise in the ratio of nonproduction to production workers in U.S. manufacturing predominantly reflected shifts *within* rather than between industries. Likewise, Bound and George Johnson find that trade basically played no role in America's wage changes in the 1980s; they ascribe those changes to technological change and changes in unmeasured labor quality. Stephen Machin finds that in the United Kingdom within-industry changes are overwhelmingly important in the rise in the ratio of nonmanual to manual workers, and Berman, Machin, and

Table 3-1. *Regressions of Price Changes on Ratios of Production to Nonproduction Workers in Japan and Germany, 1980–90*[a]

Regression	Dependent variable[b]	Constant	JP/NP[c]	GM/ NM[d]	R-square	F-statistic	Number of observations
		Wholesale prices					
1	%WP	− 14.407	5.919		0.1599	3.43	20
		(− 1.982)	(1.851)				
2	%WP	− 11.197		11.896	0.3547	8.24	17
		(− 1.109)		(2.871)			
		Import prices					
1	%MP	− 29.906	6.653		0.067	1.29	20
		(− 2.248)	(1.137)				
2	%MP	6.399		3.12	0.045	1.02	24
		(0.789)		(1.012)			

Sources: Eurostat (1992); Ministry of Labor (Japan), *December 1989 Survey* (Tokyo, 1989); Bank of Japan, Research and Statistics Department, *Price Indexes Annual*, 1980, 1985, 1990; Statistisches Bundesamt Wiesbaden, Reihe 8: *Preise und Preisindizes fuer die Ein- und Ausfuhr*, 1980, 1985, 1990; Statistisches Bundesamt Wiesbaden, Reihe 6: *Index der Grosshandelsverkaufpreise*, 1980, 1985, 1990.
a. Industry data generally correspond to SITC two-digit industries. T-statistics are in parentheses.
b. %WP = percent change in wholesale prices; %MP = percent change in import prices.
c. JP/NP = Japanese ratio of production to nonproduction workers.
d. GM/NM = German ratio of manual to nonmanual workers.

Bound reach similar conclusions after examining evidence from many more countries.[6]

I should stress, however, that the Lawrence and Slaughter paper was designed to examine the role of Stolper-Samuelson effects in trade and not, directly, to provide evidence on technological change. Moreover, since we only examined data for the manufacturing sector, we could not resolve the full role played by technology or other factors in economywide wage behavior.

For this book I have undertaken similar investigations of the price behavior of both German and Japanese imports and producer prices. Though not as disaggregated as those for the United States, these data provide similar results. As shown in table 3-1, when price changes over the 1980s are regressed against the ratio of unskilled to skilled employment, they show a *positive* rather than a negative relationship (one that is statistically significant for wholesale prices but not for import prices). Similarly, as shown in table 3-2 for both countries, when industry wholesale and import prices are weighted by production-worker shares, they show larger increases (or smaller declines) than when weighted by non-

6. Berman, Bound, and Griliches (1992); Bound and Johnson (1992); Machin (1994).

Table 3-2. *Employment-Weighted Percent Changes in Wholesale and Import Prices for Japan and Germany, 1980–90*[a]

Item	Wholesale prices	Import prices
	Japan	
All manufacturing industries		
Nonproduction industries	−5.60	−18.23
Production weights	−3.90	−17.29
Difference[b]	1.70	0.94
Without office machines		
Nonproduction weights	−7.09	−18.69
Production weights	−4.72	−17.50
Difference[b]	2.37	1.19
Without petroleum products		
Nonproduction weights	−5.49	−18.02
Production weights	−3.84	−17.19
Difference[b]	1.65	0.83
Without office machines and petroleum products		
Nonproduction weights	−6.98	−18.45
Production weights	−4.66	−17.39
Difference[b]	2.32	1.06
	Germany	
All manufacturing industries		
Nonmanual weights	23.98	15.24
Manual weights	26.03	17.07
Difference[c]	2.05	1.83
Without office machines		
Nonmanual weights	24.79	15.38
Manual weights	26.21	17.11
Difference[c]	1.42	1.73
Without petroleum products		
Nonmanual weights	24.15	15.55
Manual weights	26.11	17.20
Difference[c]	1.96	1.65
Without office machines and petroleum products		
Nonmanual weights	24.97	15.70
Manual weights	26.28	17.24
Difference[c]	1.31	1.54

Source: See table 3-1.

a. Nonproduction and nonmanual weights weigh each industry's price change by that industry's share of total manufacturing employment of nonproduction and nonmanual labor. Production and manual weights weigh each industry's price change by that industry's share of total manufacturing employment of production and manual labor. Industry data generally correspond to SITC two-digit classification.

b. Production minus nonproduction weights.

c. Manual minus nonmanual weights.

production workers.[7] For Germany I was also able to obtain unit-value data that could be matched with industry data at a more disaggregated level. Again, the data indicate no decline in the relative price of manual-worker-intensive products. In sum, in these three countries there is no evidence in either the trade or domestic price data that would lend support to the Stolper-Samuelson explanation for relative wage behavior.[8]

Critiques of Lawrence and Slaughter

Our 1993 paper has been criticized by several authors. Some have argued that our finding of a rapid increase in the ratio of skilled to unskilled workers simply reflects the fact that the relative supply of skilled workers increased rapidly in the 1980s.[9] But, as we and Berman, Bound, and Griliches have emphasized, the shift occurred *within* most industries and not only in the aggregate.[10] An important result of the Hecksher-Ohlin framework, the Rybczynski theorem, establishes that, given product prices, an increase in the supply of skilled workers raises the supply of skill-intensive goods but does not change the ratios of skilled and unskilled workers employed in each industry. Further, if this relative supply was important in changing relative product prices, it should have been associated with a *decline* in the relative wages of skilled workers— exactly the opposite of what happened. The fact that manufacturers are using more skilled labor *despite* its relatively higher price strongly supports the hypothesis that technological change in manufacturing played a role in the wage change.

Price Data

Jeffrey Sachs and Howard Shatz have raised questions about our use of the price data.[11] In particular, they argue that computer prices should

7. Questions might be raised, since these data reflect industrial classification systems that include refined petroleum as a manufactured product. In addition, it is problematic to measure the prices of products such as computers in which technological change in particularly rapid. However, as reported in table 3-2, for the weighted averages, dropping these observations does not affect the results.

8. The French case may be different. In particular, Neven and Wyplosz (1994) find a weak negative relationship between changes in industry relative prices and initial industry wages for France.

9. See, for example, Cepii (1994).

10. The Rybcynski theorem in trade theory states that, given product prices, changes in relative factor supplies affect relative product supplies rather than relative factor use.

11. Sachs and Shatz (1994).

not be included in the sample. When they drop computers, they obtain a negative but statistically insignificant relationship between import price changes and skill intensity, although they note that the size of the effect is small. Similarly, if computer price changes are omitted, instead of rising slightly the ratio of manufacturing producer prices weighted by production-worker employment to prices weighted by non-production workers falls slightly. Although Slaughter and I would agree that computer prices are difficult to measure, we are not convinced that this sector should be given no weight in the explanation. If computers are given at least some weight, there is little change in relative prices.

Edward Leamer challenges the evidence that relative prices of labor-intensive products have not fallen, but he does so over a period different from the one we examined.[12] In particular, Leamer finds evidence that the relative price of labor-intensive products declined in the 1970s. He confirms that in the 1980s, the period we examined, and the period in which the wage premiums for skilled workers increased, relative prices of labor-intensive products did not fall. Richard Cooper, who pays particular attention to the relative prices of clothing and footwear, finds that these did not decline in the 1980s.[13]

Production Worker Classification

Leamer and several other commentators have argued that the use of production and nonproduction workers as proxies for skill levels is misleading, because nonproduction workers include low-skill occupations such as secretaries, while production workers include supervisors with considerable skill. Gary Burtless points out that, in fact, the ratio of nonproduction to production worker wages has not increased as sharply as that of college to high-school graduates.[14] Indeed, as seen in table 3-1, over the 1980s the ratio of college to high-school wages in the United States increased by 15 percent, while the ratio of nonproduction to production wages increased by just 7 percent (table 3-3). This raises the

12. Leamer (forthcoming).
13. Cooper (1993). Krueger (1995), by contrast, examining the period 1989 to 1995, does find evidence that product prices have grown relatively less in sectors that use less-skilled labor more intensively. But this evidence applies to the period after the emergence of wage inequality in the United States. Moreover, in the 1990s the drift toward inequality has slowed substantially.
14. Burtless (1995).

Table 3-3. *Wage*[a] *Changes in U.S. Manufacturing, 1978–90*[b]

	Manufacturing				Manufacturing	
	All		Durables		Production	Nonproduction
Item	HS	COL	HS	COL	(hourly)	(hourly)
1978	251.45	361.43	266.87	373.07	12.40	18.98
1990	403.25	667.16	423.39	693.74	22.44	36.80
1978–90	1.60	1.85	1.59	1.86	1.81	1.94
Ratio of COL to HS	. . .	1.15	. . .	1.17	. . .	1.07

Source: CPS tapes.
a. Full-time weekly earnings.
b. HS = workers with high-school education or less. COL = workers with some college education.

possibility that the production-nonproduction worker distinction may not
be fine enough to capture the effects we are trying to explore.

For this book, therefore, I use a classification scheme based on educational attainment. Workers are divided into two categories, those with
high-school diplomas or less and those with some college experience.[15] I
have repeated regression and price-weighting exercises that are similar
to those in the original Lawrence and Slaughter analysis.[16]

As reported in table 3-4, there is no evidence that the relative price
of high-school labor-intensive products declined over the 1980s. When
import, export, and domestic price data are weighted by shares of 1979
high-school employment, they show larger price increases than when
weighted by shares of college employment. When computer price changes
are omitted, the trade prices again show a relative increase in the price
of labor-intensive goods, while domestic prices show a relative price

15. I am indebted to Jeffery Sachs and Howard Shatz for providing me with these data.
16. The U.S. Bureau of Labor Statistics began collecting trade price data in 1980.
However, in the early years of the 1980s its coverage was partial. In a period of inflation,
price changes over longer periods of time will tend to be larger. For those interested in
price changes over the 1980s as a whole there are several choices. One approach is to use
only those price data that are available for the full period. A second approach is to add in
the additional series as they become available. In Lawrence and Slaughter we adopted the
latter procedure, making the assumption that there was no bias toward the provision of
either skilled- or unskilled-labor products in the data that were made available earlier.
Sachs and Shatz were critical of this procedure and preferred to use only those prices that
were available for the complete period. But, in fact, the skill intensity of the mix of prices
available from the 1980s was similar to that for the manufacturing sector as a whole and
actually included a slightly higher share of skilled-labor-intensive products in the earlier
years, a practice that would have biased us toward finding a rise in their relative prices.
Nonetheless, in what follows, I report an analysis on trade price data using only the price
data that are available for the decade as a whole. Fully comprehensive shipments deflators
are available for the full period, and these have also been used in the analysis.

Table 3-4. *Changes in U.S. Prices Weighted by High-School and College Employment, 1980–90*

Percent

Employment	Total			Without computers		
	Imports	Exports	Domestic	Imports	Exports	Domestic
High school	29.55	43.2	29.63	29.32	43.77	30.56
College	27.46	40.1	27.96	26.88	41.65	31.2
Difference	2.09	3.1	1.67	2.64	2.12	−0.64

Source: U.S. manufactured trade prices from the Bureau of Labor Statistics.

decline of about half of 1 percent. Thus, once again, if computer prices are given some weight, there are almost no differences in this comprehensive measure.

It is also useful to undertake a regression analysis of the price changes over the decade against the initial ratios of college to high-school employment. If there were Stolper-Samuelson effects at work, one would expect to find a positive and statistically significant coefficient. Higher shares of college workers would be associated with larger price increases. As reported in table 3-5, when computer prices are excluded from the sample, with both import and export prices the coefficient is negative, although it is not statistically significant. For domestic prices it is positive although, again, not statistically significant. Without excluding computers, the coefficients are negative and statistically significant for exports and imports and almost significant for domestic prices (*t*-ratio 1.65). In sum, there is simply no support in the price analysis for a conventional Stolper-Samuelson explanation.

The U.S. data on employment by education even more strongly reinforce the evidence of skill-using technological and organizational change conveyed by the data on production and nonproduction workers. They show that in U.S. manufacturing the rapid increase in nonproduction workers was concentrated in the more highly educated professional and managerial categories. Between 1983 and 1990, for example, manufacturing employment of managers and administrators increased by 25.9 percent and professionals by 12.9 percent, whereas employment of non-sales white-collar workers declined by 3.0 percent. Although the overall share of manufacturing in total U.S. employment declined from 23 to 20 percent, the share of manufacturing in employment of managers and college-educated workers increased (from 3.9 and 3.0 percent to 4.2 and 3.6 percent, respectively). These changes are considerably more dramatic

Table 3-5. *Regressions of Price Changes on Ratios of College to HS Workers in U.S. Manufacturing, 1980–90*

Regression	Dependent variable[a]	Constant	COL/HS[b]	DCOMP[c]	R-square	F-stat	Number of observations
				Domestic prices			
1	%WP	0.29	0.056	-1.276	0.32	32.71	143
	Standard error	0.026	0.057	0.162	...	...	...
2	%WP	0.34	-0.102	...	0.018	2.52	143
	Standard error	0.03	0.064	...	...	...	...
				Import prices			
1	%MP	0.32	-0.153	-1.02	0.8	54.3	30
	Standard error	0.047	0.120	0.16	...	...	...
2	%MP	.05	-0.69	...	0.530	32	30
	Standard error	0.056	0.122	...	...	...	...
				Export prices			
1	%XP	0.36	-0.14	-1.08	0.814	37.26	20
	Standard error	0.09	0.186	0.226	...	...	...
2	%XP	0.64	-0.83	...	0.567	23.63	20
	Standard error	0.090	0.17	...	...	...	...

Sources: Current Population survey tapes as estimated by Sachs and Shatz (unpublished).
a. %WP = percent change in wholesale prices (in logs); %MP = percent change in import prices (in logs); %XP = percent change in export prices (in logs).
COL/HS = ratio of workers with high-school education or less to workers with some college education.
DCOMP = dummy variable for computer industry.

Table 3-6. *Changes in Ratio of Production-Worker Employment to Nonproduction-Worker Employment, United States, 1959–89*

	Weighted average ratios			Decomposition of change (percent)[a]	
Year	Value	Change	Percent change	Between industries	Within industries
1959	3.23	. . .	. . .	. . .	. . .
1969	3.00	(0.22)	−6.91	25.1	74.9
1979	2.79	(0.22)	−7.23	−5.9	105.9
1989	2.27	(0.51)	−18.47	30.3	69.7
1959–89	. . .	(0.95)	−29.6	−50.6	150.6

Source: NBER databank.

a. Based on the following standard decomposing formula: total change (industry x) = (change in employment share × mean production-nonproduction ratio in period) + (change in production-nonproduction ratio × mean employment share for period).

than those for production and nonproduction workers. Indeed, while employment of production workers in U.S. manufacturing declined by 14.9 percent between 1978 and 1990, employment of those with a high-school education or less declined by 21.3 percent. On the other hand, while employment of nonproduction workers increased by 8.7 percent, employment of college-educated workers increased by 23 percent.

Ratio of Skilled to Unskilled Labor

Lawrence Mishel and Jared Bernstein question whether the shift toward the relatively more intensive use of skilled labor in the 1980s is any greater than it was in earlier decades.[17] In fact it was. The shift toward the more intensive use of nonproduction workers in the 1980s was both larger and more pervasive than in the 1970s and 1960s (table 3-6).[18] The ratio of production to nonproduction workers decreased in 87 percent of the three-digit SIC codes in the 1980s, compared with 78 percent in the 1970s and 62 percent in the 1960s. Further, the average decrease was 18.5 percent in the 1980s as opposed to 6.9 percent and 7.2 percent in the 1960s and 1970s, respectively. Of course an increase on the manufacturing average could reflect either a change in the mix of industries or in the ratio within industries. As table 3-6 shows, both factors were at work.

17. Mishel and Bernstein (1994).
18. Though perhaps not larger than in the 1950s. Sachs and Shatz (1994) show a rapid increase between 1947 and 1960.

The skill-intensive-sector share of employment increased and the within-sector shares of skilled labor in employment increased. However, 70 percent of the shift occurred within industries. Since this shift occurred even though the relative wages of nonproduction workers increased, it appears to be strongly suggestive of a skilled-labor-using technological and organizational shift.

Technological Change

Mishel and Bernstein also raise the question whether the change in skill intensity should be described as technological change. In particular, they find an absence of evidence showing an association with investment and other hard measures of technical change, such as research and development (R&D), capital accumulation, and computerization, and stress the importance of distinguishing developments in manufacturing from those in the rest of the economy.[19]

I believe both the points they make are important. First, if this evidence is correct, those arguing for a major role for technology must apply a broader interpretation that includes new labor-management relations and work organization. Indeed, there is considerable evidence that manufacturing production technologies are undergoing a massive change from systems based on Fordist mass-production techniques toward a new post-Fordist paradigm that places a much greater emphasis on flexibility, learning, and skills.[20] Second, I believe the divergent productivity performance between the manufacturing and service sectors in the United States was a major structural feature of the U.S. economy in the 1980s. Historically, relative productivity growth was faster in goods than in services. But this difference widened in the 1980s, when almost all the improvements in total factor productivity in the business sector were confined to manufacturing. If the demand for manufacturing goods is inelastic, relatively rapid increases in manufacturing productivity will reduce the demand for manufacturing workers. With no bias in this change, since production workers are relatively intensively employed in manufacturing, that will reduce the demand for production workers. In

19. Allen (1993) finds that variations in innovative activity do affect relative industry wages and, in particular, that there is a positive association between returns to schooling and R&D spending.

20. See Boyer (1995) for a more detailed description, and Oman (1996) for a discussion of the implication of the new paradigm for globalization.

combination with a shift within manufacturing toward production-worker-saving technical change concentrated in nonproduction worker sectors, the impact on relative wages could be considerable.

Whatever its source, relative prices will obviously be affected by this combination of technological and organizational change. In the traditional Stolper-Samuelson story, technology is assumed to remain constant, but in the real world technology clearly does not. Even if the increased supply of products from developing countries was exerting a downward pressure on the relative wages of unskilled workers, at the same time this pressure was possibly offset by relatively rapid increases in technological change in skill-intensive sectors.

Leamer has questioned the relevance of skill-biased technical change as an explanation for growing wage inequality. He notes that in the conventional Stolper-Samuelson world, in which world prices are given, relative wages are affected by the sector in which progress is dominant rather than the bias of the technological change.[21] But in any case, the evidence on the sectoral incidence of the technological change is only relevant in the context of a model in which the economy is small and the technological change is purely domestic. As Krugman emphasizes, both the bias and the sectoral location of technological change could matter if the technology shock was global, if the economy was specialized, or if product demand was not infinitely elastic.[22] In Lawrence and Slaughter we concluded that in the United States total factor productivity (TFP) growth had been relatively rapid in the skill-intense sectors. But Sachs and Shatz found on the basis of their regression omitting the computer industry that there was a negative relationship between TFP growth and skill intensity. They conclude that "TFP growth was less on average in high-skilled than low-skilled industries" and argue, therefore, that technological change was causing wage differentials to narrow rather than widen—implying a greater role for trade.[23] Again, the impact of the computer industry is important. In Lawrence and Slaughter we found that, including computers, the gap between weighted averages of high-skilled and low-skilled productivity growth was positive and thus concluded the impact was the opposite. From the standpoint of economic theory, it is hard to understand why the effect of the computer industry should be ignored.

21. Leamer (forthcoming).
22. Krugman (1995a).
23. Sachs and Shatz (1994, p. 39).

Trade and Technology

There remains the issue whether technological change itself has been affected by trade. Indeed, as noted in chapter 2, this point is stressed in particular by Wood.[24] But the links between international competition and technological change are complex.[25] In general, investment in technological change is stimulated by anticipated profits. If import competition depresses the returns in certain industries, one would expect *less* rather than more technological changes in such activities. In addition, scale is an important factor in the returns to R&D spending, since research has a substantial fixed-cost component. Again, one would expect *less* R&D spending in import-competing sectors (although export sectors would have the opposite effects). However, competition and exposure to superior foreign firms could also speed up technological acquisition and thus lead to faster technological change because of emulation. But one would not expect technological changes in developed countries to use more capital-intensive production methods when experiencing competition from developing countries. If the relative price of unskilled workers falls, one would expect technological change to save on other factors and to use unskilled labor more intensively rather than the reverse. Also, to the degree that increased import competition with labor-intensive products operates through Stolper-Samuelson effects to raise the relative cost of skilled and educated workers, it could make R&D relatively more expensive. For all these reasons, therefore, one would not anticipate that the effect of trade with developing countries would be to speed up technological change in the labor-intensive sectors, especially with a view to saving on unskilled labor.

There are paradigms, however, that are different from those of traditional profit maximization, in which managers may be stimulated to innovate when international competition threatens their rents. This involves

24. Wood (1994). Sachs and Shatz (1994) found that during 1960–78 TFP growth was slightly lower on average in low-skill (that is, production-worker-intensive) industries than in high-skill ones; during 1978–90, however, it was slightly greater in low-skill sectors. The bottom decile had virtually no growth in TFP on an annual basis, while the top decile experienced a slow down of 0.8 percent a year. Wood (1995) interprets this as support for his hypothesis. But though relative TFP growth is important in determining relative wages, it is not clear why this is an appropriate measure of the impact of trade with developing countries.

25. For a discussion, see Binswanger (1974).

shifts in so-called X-inefficiency, in which firms behave under conditions of what is sometimes termed bounded rationality. Basically, they do not innovate continuously but do so when subject to an unusual stimulus.

Using detailed case studies and more general regression analysis, F. M. Scherer has studied the R&D spending responses of U.S. firms to international competition.[26] He finds a mixture of responses. Some firms aggressively innovated in the face of competition; others simply submitted. On average, in the short run R&D-to-sales ratios declined. Companies were more aggressive the greater their domestic sales, the more concentrated the markets in which they competed, and the more diversified their domestic operations. Companies with only U.S. operations were more submissive than those that were multinationals.

These considerations suggest that responses to trade could be different, depending on the degree of competition in the market. Indeed, James MacDonald finds that in the United States increases in import competition led to large statistically significant increases in labor productivity growth in highly concentrated industries but not in other industries.[27] Since OECD imports from developing countries typically occur in sectors that are highly competitive, such as apparel and leather, it is less likely that the technology-inducing effects of trade will be significant. By contrast, these effects may be more important for trade with developed countries, more of which occurs in concentrated sectors. In the U.S. case, therefore, the MacDonald findings suggest that increased trade competition might actually have induced an acceleration in technological change in concentrated and skill-intensive sectors, an effect that for a small price-taking economy is exactly the opposite of the one Wood believes to have been important. Indeed, given product prices, disproportionately rapid technological change in the skill-intensive sectors will increase the relative wage of skilled workers.[28]

In sum, therefore, trade could have had a role in stimulated technological change and thus adversely affected the relative wages of unskilled workers, but the impact is more likely to have occurred through the inducing of unusually rapid growth in the high-skill sector rather than the reverse.

26. Scherer (1992).
27. MacDonald (1994).
28. See Leamer (forthcoming).

Quantifying the Effects

In this and the previous chapter, I have noted three important factors that seem to have had an adverse effect on the relative wages of U.S. workers with a high-school education or less. The first is international trade. The second is deindustrialization: shifts in demand patterns due both to trade and other factors combined with relatively rapid productivity growth in manufacturing have led to a declining share of manufacturing employment in the economy. The third factor is skill-biased technical and organizational change. In this section I try a rather crude approach to use a shift-share analysis to answer two questions. First, what is the relative importance of these effects, and second, taken together, can these effects account for a significant share of the growing inequality that took place in the United States in the 1980s, a change of about 15 percent in the ratio of wages of workers with a high-school education or less to those with some college education or more?

Table 3-7 reports estimates of the relative demand for workers with different levels of education under different calculations. The first calculation repeats the estimate of the impact of trade reported earlier. Estimates from Sachs and Shatz of the effect of trade on employment in two-digit manufacturing are combined with data on the relative employment of high-school and college workers, by industry, to estimate the effect of trade on high-school and college employment. This conventional net-factor estimate suggests that without the trade changes over the 1980s—actually those between 1978 and 1990—the share of workers with a high-school education in manufacturing in 1990 would have been 61.2 percent rather than 60 percent. Without trade, the manufacturing sector would have increased its demand for workers with a high-school education by 939,000, which was equal to 1.8 percent of all such workers in the United States in 1990. Similarly, demand for workers with some college education would have increased by 0.47 percent. The net increase in overall relative high-school demand, therefore, would have been 1.3 percent. If the demand for different types of labor has a unitary elasticity, under this scenario relative earnings of unskilled workers throughout the economy would have been higher by 1.3 percent.

The second calculation estimates the effects of deindustrialization: the total decline in the share of manufacturing in overall employment, regardless of its source. This estimate therefore captures the effect of trade and other demand factors as well as the relatively rapid productivity

Table 3-7. *Impact of Trade, Deindustrialization, and Skill-Labor Substitution on Employment over the 1980s, Alternative Calculations*
Employment and demand in thousands

Calculation	High school		College
1. Impact of trade			
Net change in demand	939.00		255.00
Percent of 1990 total employment	1.83		0.47
Implied change in HS/COL ratio (percent)		**1.35**	
2. Impact of deindustrialization[a]			
In 1990 nonmanufacturing employment down			
0.058 percent of total, or 6,091.856	2,826.62		3,265.23
In 1990 manufacturing employment up by			
0.058 percent of total, or 6,091.856	3,661.21		2,430.65
Hypothetical employment with 1980			
manufacturing share			
Net change in demand	834.58		− 834.58
As percent of total high school	1.63		. . .
As percent of total college	. . .		− 1.55
Implied change in HS/COL ratio (percent)		**3.23**	
3. Impact of technological change[b]			
1990 manufacturing employment	13,112.66		5,566.34
Net change in demand	1,886.58		− 1,886.58
As percent of total high school	3.68		. . .
As percent of total college	. . .		− 3.51
Implied change in HS/COL ratio (percent)		**7.5**	
4. Impact of 2 and 3[c]			
Manufacturing employment	17,339.60		7,431.26
Nonmanufacturing employment	36,912.45		43,332.00
Total hypothetical demand	54,252.05		50,763.26
Actual 1990 employment	51,293.87		53,738.13
Difference (percent)	5.77		− 5.54
Implied change in HS/COL ratio (percent)		**11.97**	

Addenda: Full-time employment

					Manufacturing				
Year	Total	HS	COL	HS/COL	Total	Share	HS	COL	HS/COL
1979	87,400	51,002.82	34,593.94	1.47	20,613	0.24	14,470.33	6,142.67	0.70
1990	105,032	51,293.87	53,738.13	0.95	18,679	0.18	11,226.08	7,452.92	0.60

Sources: Full-time employment from National Income Accounts; impact of trade: estimates of Sachs and Shatz (1994) and CPS estimates of college and high-school employment; shares of high-school and college from CPS March surveys.
a. Assume manufacturing share of employment at 1980 level (23.6 percent); ratio of high-school to college workers at 1990 level (.60).
b. Assume manufacturing share of employment at 1990 level (17.8 percent); ratio of high-school to college workers at 1980 level (.70).
c. Assume manufacturing share of employment at 1980 level (23.6 percent); ratio of high-school to college workers at 1980 level (.70).

growth in manufacturing. Since employment in U.S. manufacturing is concentrated among workers with a high-school education or less, deindustrialization has an adverse impact on the demand for high-school workers.[29] The second calculation investigates the impact in 1990 if the employment share in manufacturing had remained at its 1979 level of 23.6 percent instead of its actual share of 17.8 percent. The ratios of workers with some college education to high-school workers in manufacturing and nonmanufacturing are assumed to be at 1990 levels. Manufacturing is relatively more intensive in high-school employment. Assuming 1990 factor proportions but increasing the share of employment in manufacturing raises the demand for high-school workers by 1.6 percent and reduces the demand for workers with some college education by 1.6 percent. This implies a shift in relative demand of 3.2 percent. If the elasticity of substitution between high-school and college workers is unity, given actual supplies, that would induce a proportionate change in relative wages. This therefore suggests that, overall, deindustrialization had an effect that was two and a half times as large as trade and that the factors besides trade, such as relatively faster productivity growth, had an effect about one and a half times as large as trade.

The third calculation crudely estimates the effects of skill-biased technological and organizational change. The shares of employment between the manufacturing and nonmanufacturing sectors are kept at their 1990 levels, but the ratio of high-school to college employment in manufacturing is raised to its 1979 level. Assuming no change in the output mix of the manufacturing sector, this can be thought of as an estimate of the change in the relative demand for factors induced by high-school-substituting technological and organizational change under the assumption of zero elasticities of substitution. Without this shift, 1.9 million more high-school workers would have been demanded in manufacturing and a similar number of college workers would not have been. In all, the relative increase in relative demand for high-school workers would have been 7.2 percent larger, a shock that is of a considerable order of magnitude and more than twice as large as the impact due to deindustrialization and more than five times the size of the impact of trade. Moreover, it is likely that this crude procedure underestimates the impact of the technological and organizational change because, by using actual 1990

29. In 1979, according to Sachs and Shatz (forthcoming), these workers made up 70.2 percent of full-time manufacturing employment. According to Davis and Haltiwanger (1991), in 1979–81 the share was 71.48 percent. By 1990 the share had fallen to 60.1 percent.

shares, it ignores the impact of the higher relative wages of college workers in inducing substitution of high-school for college workers. On the other hand, shifts in the composition of manufacturing output due to shifts in demand could also account for some of the rise. Indeed, as reported in table 3-6, between-industry shifts accounted for about 30 percent of the change in overall reduction in the ratio of production to nonproduction workers.

Calculation four combines the effects of deindustrialization and biased technological and organizational change by holding both the share of manufacturing in total employment and the ratio of high-school to college workers at their 1979 levels. Under these circumstances, the demand for high-school workers is raised by 5.8 percent and the demand for college workers declines by 5. 5 percent. All told, therefore, under these circumstances there would be a 12 percent increase in the ratio of high-school to college graduates, a shock that would have an appreciable effect on relative college wages. Indeed, if the elasticity of substitution is unity, the change in relative wages would be 12 percent. *Together, therefore, these changes could account for about three-quarters of the increased relative wage of college graduates in the U.S. economy as a whole.*

Of course, trade could be a reason for *both* the declining share of employment in manufacturing and for the increasing share of college to high-school workers in manufacturing. But in all the 1.3 percent effect due to trade is just over 10 percent of the total differential accounted for by these calculations. These estimates suggest, therefore, that trade played a role in reducing the relative demand for high-school workers, but the impact was considerably smaller than that of the other factors I have identified. It was about one-third the impact of deindustrialization due to fairly rapid productivity growth and about one-fifth of the impact of the shift in demand for college workers and away from high-school workers in manufacturing.

As we have seen, estimating the impact of trade on wages using the net-factor approach requires a two-step procedure. The first is to estimate the effect of net flows of factors embodied in trade on the relative-factor supplies in the economy. The second is then to estimate the effect of these changes in relative supplies on relative wages. To perform this second step, we need a measure of the elasticity of substitution between different types of workers. In general, those believing that trade has had a large effect believe this elasticity is low, that it takes a large change in relative wages to induce substitution in factor use. But if the elasticity of substitution is low, it implies not only that effects due to trade will be larger, but also that other changes shifting the relative demand curve or relative supply will have larger effects as well. Factor-content studies that argue that the effects of trade were large because of the elasticity of substitution was low would also have to conclude that the effects of relative-factor supplies and technological change were also larger, and if the estimates above were realistic, the relative importance of trade would remain low.

This exercise should be treated with care. The calculation is seriously incomplete because it ignores (1) the effects that the large increase in the relative supply of educated workers in the 1980s would have had in depressing the skill premium, and (2) the effects of skill-biased technical change in the rest of the U.S. economy. Taken together, these omissions suggest that skill-biased changes must actually have been far larger than estimated here. It has involved shift-share analysis and used proportional arithmetic rather than serious behavioral economics. The analysis is the more useful the more limited substitution possibilities between goods and factors are. Nonetheless, I hope it provides some sense of the relative orders of magnitude involved and can serve as the basis for further research. It suggests strongly that developments in U.S. manufacturing could well have been a driving force behind the growing earnings inequality in the 1980s. Although trade made a contribution, the relatively rapid increase in manufacturing productivity was more significant, and both effects were dwarfed by skill-biased technological and organizational change.

Conclusion

In this and the previous chapter, I have considered the effect of trade with developing countries on the skill premium in the United States in the context of models with competitive labor markets. However, it is hard to provide evidence that is conclusive and to find methodologies that do not require string assumptions to be applied. We know that in reality many shocks affect wages, but to use the net-factor-content approach, we need to assume that trade flows reflect only changes in the opportunities to trade. Similarly, to use price evidence, we need to assume that these reflect the impact of trade policies at home and abroad or somehow to separate the effects of technology on prices. In addition, for both methodologies we need knowledge about behavioral response, such as elasticities of factor and product demand. Nonetheless, it does appear that for the 1980s, the period in which the skill premium in the United States increased dramatically, the role of trade with developing countries was relatively small.

Appendix 3A. A Graphical Illustration of the Stolper-Samuelson Theorem

To describe the Stolper-Samuelson process, consider a small open economy that produces two products, software and textiles, with two factors, skilled and unskilled labor. *Open* means that the country freely trades both goods with the rest of the world. *Small* means that the country's production and consumption choices do not influence its terms of trade. Instead, these relative prices are determined in the rest of the world. Furthermore, suppose that software uses skilled labor relatively intensively.[30] Initially, the country settles at some equilibrium output mix of software and textiles. To produce this mix, firms employ the country's skilled and unskilled labor. The labor market generates an equilibrium wage for each type of labor; at this wage the quantity demanded by firms equals the total quantity supplied in the economy.

One can illustrate this equilibrium by choosing the production iso-quants for software and textiles that correspond to their given relative price. In figure 3A-1a these are drawn as SS and TT, respectively. Note that SS lies above and to the left of TT. This indicates that software uses skilled labor relatively intensively. If both goods are produced, both isoquants must be tangent to the line that shows the unique ratio of factor prices (W_s/W_u). These tangency points show the ratios of skilled to unskilled labor $(S/U)_s$ and $(S/U)_t$ used to produce software and textiles, respectively.[31]

30. This is an assumption about the technology of production. It means that for any given relative wages the ratio of skilled to unskilled labor employed in making one unit of software exceeds the ratio of skilled to unskilled labor employed in making one unit of textiles. Since there are only two goods and two factors in this economy, if software uses skilled labor relatively intensively, then textiles use unskilled labor relatively intensively. We assume no factor-intensity reversals; that is, that at all factor prices software uses relatively more skilled labor.

31. If technological capabilities are the same throughout the world, and specialization is incomplete, the unique relationship between goods prices and factor prices leads to factor-price equalization.

Figure 3A-1. *The Stolper-Samuelson Process in a Small Open Economy*

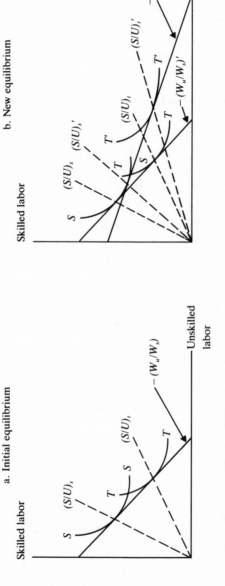

a. Initial equilibrium

Skilled labor

$(S/U)_s$

S

T

$(S/U)_t$

S

T

$-(W_u/W_s)$

Unskilled labor

b. New equilibrium

Skilled labor

$(S/U)_s$ $(S/U)_s'$

S

T

T

$(S/U)_t$

S

T

$(S/U)_t'$

T

$-(W_u/W_s)'$

$-(W_u/W_s)$

Unskilled labor

Source: Lawrence and Slaughter (1993).
Note: SS and TT are the initial production isoquants of software and textiles, respectively. $-(W_u/W_s)$ is the negative of the economy's initial relative-ware ratio. $(S/U)_s$ and $(S/U)_t$ are the initial ratios of skilled to unskilled labor employed in software and textiles, respectively.

Note: The international price of software has risen. Software output increases, and textile output shrinks. This is represented as a shift in the textile isoquant to $T'T'$. $-(W_u/W_s)$ is the negative of the economy's new relative-wage ratio: the wage of skilled labor has risen relative to unskilled labor. $(S/U)_t$ and $(S/U)_t'$ are the new ratios of skilled to (un-skilled labor employed in software and extiles, respectively.

Now suppose that the international price of software rises. This is depicted in figure 3A-1b as an outward shift in the relevant textile iso-quant to $T'T'$. The country will seek to make more software and fewer textiles. Output in textiles declines, releasing some of both factors. Output in software expands, requiring more of both factors. Because software employs skilled labor relatively intensively, the whole economy's relative demand shifts toward skilled labor and away from unskilled labor. If factor prices remained constant, however, the factor quantities released by textiles would not match those demanded by software, because of the different factor intensities of the goods. The textile industry would release too much unskilled labor and too little skilled labor relative to what the software industry demands.

Wages must therefore change. The unskilled-labor wage falls, and the skilled-labor wage rises. As drawn in figure 3A-1b, the new equilibrium relative-factor-price ratio is $(W_s/W_u)' > (W_s/W_u)$. In both parts of figure 3A-1 the curved isoquants reflect the possibility of factor substitution. Thus this higher ratio induces firms to substitute away from skilled labor toward unskilled labor, and this substitution lowers the ratio of skilled to unskilled labor employed in each industry. In figure 3A-1b this substitution is represented as a flattening of each industry's (S/U) ray to $(S/U)'$. The textile sector thus releases less unskilled labor and more skilled labor relative to what it would have released without the wage change. Similarly, software demands more unskilled labor and less skilled labor relative to what it would have released without the wage change. Wages move just enough to reemploy all labor; at this point the economy attains its new equilibrium. As Leamer emphasizes, however, the effect on relative factor prices occurs even when production takes place with fixed coefficients.[32]

32. Leamer (1994). The simple Stolper-Samuelson model can be extended by allowing either or both of the industries to be imperfectly competitive with increasing returns to scale. Helpman and Krugman (1985) find that the relative-price effect operates in models with imperfect competition, although the factor adversely affected need not experience an absolute decline in its return. The model can also be extended by increasing the number of factors of production and goods. Ethier (1984) shows that if the number of factors equals the number of goods, the model can identify after a change in a good's price the factor whose price rises in terms of every good and the factor whose price falls in terms of every good. If the number of factors does not equal the number of goods, the model cannot unambiguously identify these two factors after the price change.

Appendix 3B. Relative Wage Behavior with Specialization

There are theories that break the tight relationship between the terms of trade and relative factor prices by assuming complete specialization. These theories have the intriguing implication that the difficulties facing U.S. unskilled workers reflect the fact that there are too few very poor countries rather than too many. One version of the argument stresses the impact of international capital flows; another, the international diffusion of technology.[33] In both versions average wage rates in the rich country fall at the same time as its terms of trade decline.

In the version that emphasizes capital mobility there are three types of goods, differentiated by capital intensity. Only the rich country produces the most capital-intensive product (computers), and only the poor country produces the least capital-intensive product (textiles). Both countries produce the mid-range product (radios). Initially, the wage-rental ratio is higher in the rich than in the poor country. As capital shifts into the poor country, that country increases its production of radios. This process shifts the rich country away from the production of radios and toward computers. It also shifts the poor country away from the production of textiles and toward radios. Within the rich country, therefore, the Stolper-Samuelson mechanism operates because the relative price of radios is falling and because more labor than capital is released from the shrinking radio industry. This requires a lower wage-rental ratio to restore full employment. In the poor country, an analogous effect operates to raise the wage-rental ratio. When the countries have sufficiently similar relative factor endowments, relative factor prices converge. This model has been presented using capital and labor; however, it could readily be extended to skill, disaggregated between skilled and unskilled labor.[34]

Three-goods models with technological diffusion can generate a similar result. Consider technological change in a simple Ricardian model. The world is divided into a lead and a follower country.[35] The lead country

33. Leamer (1992) presents the first version. Collins (1985), Johnson and Stafford (1992), and Krugman (1979) present varieties of the second version.

34. In models with complete specialization, increased capital mobility need not, however, always lower the real wage of workers in the North. As Feenstra and Hanson (1994) point out, a capital outflow will lower the marginal product of northern labor in terms of its home good but will also lower the relative price of the southern good. It is possible, therefore, for the wage of northern labor to rise in terms of the southern good.

35. In Collins (1985) the argument involves three countries.

initially specializes in the two more technologically sophisticated products (computers and radios), while the follower country specializes in the least (textiles). With technological advance in radios in the follower country, production of radios shifts from the lead to the follower nation. Again, this process shifts the rich country away from the production of radios and toward computers. It also shifts the poor country away from the production of textiles and toward radios. The result is an increase in the relative price of textiles. Real wages in the lead country fall because the decline in the relative price of now-imported radios is offset by the increase in the relative price of textiles. From the standpoint of the lead country, the problem is too little production of textiles and too much production of radios.

Integrating the effects of labor-force growth, technological diffusion, and capital mobility in a single model requires considerable fortitude. This has been done by David Dollar in a model with complete specialization.[36] Dollar shows that in the short run labor-force growth in the South raises the terms of trade and the level of wages in the North. However, this rise in northern wages increases the rate of diffusion of both technology and capital to the South. This long-run effect, as has been seen, tends to worsen the North's terms of trade and equalize wages between the two regions.

Do these theories provide a better explanation of U.S. developments in the 1980s than the simple HOS model? The answer seems to be no. First, in the two-factor models with capital and labor one expects to see the terms of trade declining, the wage-rental rate falling, and product wages falling behind average productivity growth. But as reported in chapter 1, the United States recorded a marginal improvement in its terms of trade, no decline in the wage-rental ratio, and product wages that matched productivity growth. Similarly, a two-factor model with nonproduction and production workers does not predict what we actually found in Lawrence and Slaughter: constant terms of trade, the relatively similar performance of import prices using production and nonproduction worker shares as weights, and the widespread shift toward the use of nonproduction workers. Nonetheless, models with complete specialization do have the virtue of allowing for domestic relative labor supply and skill-biased technical change to play a role in relative-wage determination even in economies that are price takers in world markets.

36. Dollar (1986).

CHAPTER FOUR

The Loss of Good Jobs?

IN THE PREVIOUS chapter I argued that there does not appear to be much evidence that the Stolper-Samuelson process operated in a powerful fashion over the 1980s to bring about the growing wage dispersion seen in the United States. However, the Heckscher-Ohlin framework rests heavily on the assumptions of perfect competition and complete internal factor mobility. Under these conditions factors of production earn similar returns throughout the economy. In principle, this property of the model is attractive for explaining economywide factor returns, the phenomenon I am interested in. But factor returns may not be equalized throughout the economy if there are labor-market frictions, barriers to entry, firm-specific capital, and other market imperfections.

There is, moreover, considerable evidence that such factors have important effects on relative industry wages and result in distinctive industry premiums or rents.[1] That suggests two important possibilities. First, even if relatively unimportant in explaining economywide wage behavior, trade could be an important determinant of the wage and employment behavior of particular industries. Second, trade could affect relative economywide factor returns through an indirect route. If employment of unskilled or less-educated workers is especially concentrated in high-rent industries whose wages or employment is adversely affected by trade, the average economywide earnings of unskilled workers could fall relative to the average earnings of skilled workers.[2]

1. Katz and Summers (1989); Dickens and Lang (1988).
2. Borjas and Ramey (1993; 1994) and Murphy and Welch (1991) emphasize the cor-

78

Many tests have been made of the impact of trade on industry relative wages in the OECD and as the review of them presented in appendix 4A makes clear, they have usually yielded mixed results. There are some hints that increased trade pressures may affect relative industry wages, but in general the effects are fairly small. In particular, Ana Ravenga examined the United States in the 1980s and found some evidence of downward relative wage pressure, but the effects were not large.[3]

The work of George Borjas and Valerie Ramey is the most prominent in claiming a strong effect operating through this mechanism. They construct a partial equilibrium model that elegantly captures the relationship between union rents and trade.[4] The economy is divided into a competitive sector in which workers do not earn rents, and a unionized sector in which firms have market power and are forced by unions to share their rents with workers. Rents earned in the unionized sector thus depend on the derived labor-demand elasticity facing individual firms. This elasticity is in turn a function of industry concentration and the share of demand taken by imports. Thus rents are higher the more concentrated the industry is and the lower its share of imports. This model is useful because it rigorously demonstrates a potential link between import *volumes* and domestic relative wages.[5] If the unionized sector has a larger share of unskilled workers than the competitive sector, the decline in rents in the unionized sector could lower the economywide average relative returns to unskilled workers.

In this model, when foreign firms enter markets in the unionized sector, they lower the relative wage of unskilled workers through three effects: first, they place downward pressure on the rents of workers still employed in the industries; second, they reduce employment in the unionized sector, thereby reducing the number of unskilled workers who earn rents; third, they put downward pressure on the relative wages of

---

relation between the time trends in the trade deficit in durable goods and the log of the wage differential between college graduates and less-educated workers. Surprisingly, perhaps, Borjas and Ramey find that this association goes back to the 1950s, a period in which U.S. trade in those goods was a much less important factor in domestic competition.

3. Ravenga (1992).

4. The model is one of Cournot oligopoly, in which firms take other firms' quantities as given.

5. In empirical applications the assumption that the quantity of imports is exogenous may sometimes present a problem. But if imports were constrained by a binding quota, such as the voluntary restraint arrangements in U.S. steel and automobiles, this assumption would be perfectly plausible.

unskilled workers in the rest of the economy, since the relative supply of unskilled workers to the nonunionized sector increases.

Borjas and Ramey also provide empirical support for their model. They note that, in general, durable manufacturing industries are relatively concentrated and pay higher wages even after accounting for observable differences in worker characteristics. They point out, for example, that workers in the automobile and steel industries, about 80 percent of whom are high-school graduates or dropouts, earn about 24 percent and 16 percent more, respectively, than equally educated workers employed in other industries.

They then undertake both time-series and cross-sectional analysis. In their time-series analysis of the U.S. data they estimate that each 1 percent rise in durable goods imports as a percent of GNP raises the economywide relative wages of college graduates compared with high-school graduates by 0.39 percent and the relative wages of college graduates compared with high-school dropouts by 0.59 percent. In their cross-sectional *regional* analysis, they obtain relationships of a similar magnitude: each 10 percentage point increase in the share of manufacturing employment in a region decreases the college premium (over high-school wages) by about 2 to 4 percentage points. These are sizable effects. If one assumes that all the change is simply due to the loss of given rents earned by workers in manufacturing, one would obtain such a result only if just unskilled workers were employed in manufacturing and earned a 20–40 percent premium over similar workers employed in competitive industries.

Borjas and Ramey suggest that *the entire decline in the share of employment* in what they term high-concentration import industries can serve as a "very rough proxy for the impact of foreign competition on the wage structure."[6] Assuming a 40 percent premium, they argue that the decline in the employment share in these industries in 1976–90 from 7.3 percent to 4.2 percent accounts (3.1 × 0.4) for a 1.3 percent decline in the relative, economywide wage of high-school graduates. As a result, they claim that about 10 percent of the total decline of about 13 percent in the ratio of high-school wages to college-graduate wages in their sample is due to these effects.

These orders of magnitude, however, are subject to question. In the first place Borjas and Ramey's work uses a reduced-form relationship

6. Borjas and Ramey (1993, p. 25).

Table 4-1. *Changes in Earnings in Manufacturing, Durable Goods, and Concentrated Industries, 1979–90*
Average weekly earnings (dollars)

Year	Durables (1)	Concentrated (2)	Manufacturing (3)	(2)/(3)	Employment share of concentrated
			High-school workers		
1979	266.87	303.10	251.45	1.21	0.20
1990	423.39	476.37	403.25	1.18	0.18
1990/1979	1.57	1.57	1.60	. . .	. . .
			College workers		
1979	373.07	397.48	381.43	1.10	0.25
1990	693.74	731.08	667.18	1.10	0.24
1990/1979	1.84	1.84	1.85	. . .	. . .

Sources: CPS tapes; concentrated industries as defined by Borjas and Ramey (1993).

that does not account separately for the different channels they have identified. If trade is an important source of inequality, does it operate by shifting the composition of employment and thus the availability of high-rent jobs? Does it operate by placing downward pressure on the rents of workers employed in such industries? Or does it operate simply by adding to the supply of displaced workers who need then to be reemployed in the rest of the economy? In what follows, I offer evidence on each of these questions in turn.

Trade and the Level of Rents

Has trade actually resulted in downward pressure on industry rents? Lawrence Katz and Lawrence Summers estimated the industry rents earned by workers in the United States in 1984.[7] Their results confirm that these rents are particularly high in manufacturing in general and in durable goods industries such as transportation and primary metals in particular. It is instructive to compare changes in earnings in high-rent industries with those in the rest of the economy. Table 4-1 reports such changes for three groups of workers: manufacturing, durable manufacturing, and the group of highly concentrated industries that Borjas and Ramey categorize as "highly concentrated import competing."[8] In 1978, on average, workers with a high-school education earned $267 a week,

7. Katz and Summers (1989).
8. Borjas and Ramey (1993, pp. 19–20).

as against $251 for manufacturing as a whole. By contrast, average earnings of such workers in concentrated industries were $303, or more than 20 percent above the manufacturing average, numbers that roughly accord with the Borjas-Ramey figures for automobiles.

But have these premiums actually been depressed as implied by Borjas and Ramey? It appears they have not. Between 1979 and 1990 earnings of high-school workers in durable goods, manufacturing, and highly concentrated goods increased by 59, 60, and 57 percent, respectively. The relative wage in concentrated sectors declined by just 2 percent, mainly because of wage declines in primary metals. Earnings of high-school workers in textiles and apparel, the main low-rent sectors, actually increased as rapidly as those in transportation, chemicals, and refined petroleum. With the notable exception of primary metals, no decline is apparent in relative earnings in major high-rent sectors. A decline of rents of 2 percent for 7 percent of U.S. workers can only explain a shift of 0.14 percent, about a tenth the size of the effect found by Borjas and Ramey. Hence this channel does not appear to explain much of the total shift in the wage distribution.

Trade and the Availability of Rents

A second channel relates to the impact of trade on the composition of employment. The net-factor-content approach is useful in providing an estimate of the actual employment shifts due to trade, taking wages and their associated premiums as given. Jeffrey Sachs and Howard Shatz have used the net-factor-content approach to estimate the effect of trade on U.S. manufacturing employment. They have also provided separate estimates of the impact of trade with developed and developing countries on employment by two-digit industries. In what follows, therefore, I use their estimates of counterfactual employment behavior in the absence of changes in trade.[9]

Katz and Summers report the rents earned by managers and laborers in 1984 in each two-digit industry.[10] I assume the rents they estimate for each industry that are earned by managers are representative of rents earned by nonproduction and college-educated workers. Similarly, I assume the rents earned by laborers are representative of those earned by

9. Sachs and Shatz (1994).
10. Katz and Summers (1989).

Table 4-2. *Impact of Compositional Changes on Worker Rents in U.S. Manufacturing, 1978–90*

Item	Average rents for workers in manufacturing			
	High school	College	Production	Nonproduction
1978 (1)	6.90	11.30	7.22	10.90
1990 (2)	6.62	11.30	7.22	10.83
No trade, 1990 (3)	5.86	11.11	6.48	10.66
Trade impact (3 − 2)	−0.76	−0.18	−0.74	−0.17

Sources: Calculated using rents for managers and laborers in 1984 from Katz and Summers (1989) and Sachs and Shatz (1994) counterfactual scenario.

production workers and workers with a high-school education or less. I can thus compute the employment-weighted average rents earned by different types of workers in 1978 and 1990. The results of this calculation are reported in table 4-2. In addition, by using the Sachs-Shatz counterfactual scenario, I can also estimate the impact of trade in general and with the developing countries in particular.

The data reported in table 4-2 show that the share of manufacturing employment in high- and low-rent industries did not shift much over the decade. The average rents earned by production and high-school workers in 1978 (6.9 and 7.5 percent, respectively) are remarkably similar to those earned in 1990 (6.7 and 7.2 percent). The same is true of the higher rents earned by managers and college graduates (roughly 11 percent). Thus within U.S. manufacturing low- and high-rent jobs were lost at quite similar rates over this period.

According to the Shatz and Sachs estimates, without trade high-school employment in manufacturing would have been higher by 6.8 percent. Interestingly, however, average rents within manufacturing for such workers would have been slightly lower. That is because the sectors on which trade had the largest impact were those such as textiles and apparel in which rents are low or negative. On average, had they not been displaced as a result of trade, workers in manufacturing would have earned rents equal to 5.9 percent, as against the 6.6 percent it is estimated they earned.

Thus trade actually raised the average of the remaining high-rent jobs in manufacturing. As a result of trade, however, fewer workers were able to obtain employment in manufacturing. In 1990, for example, 21.9 percent of high-school workers in the United States were employed in manufacturing. With counterfactual trade, the share of total employment of such workers in manufacturing would have been about 2 percentage points higher. If these workers were required to work in the rest of the economy, where they earned no rents at all, this means that the loss of high-rent manufacturing jobs lowered average high-school workers' wages by 0.02×6.9, or about 0.1 of 1 percent, a quite negligible amount that must be counterbalanced against the reduction in average rents that no trade would have induced within manufacturing. Moreover, in the counterfactual trade scenario, employment would also have been higher for managers and college-educated workers, so the impact on the *relative* wage would have been even smaller.

The third channel would simply be the relative wage decline required to absorb workers displaced as a result of trade into the rest of the economy. The estimates using the input-output analysis suggest that these numbers are small. As reported in table 2-1, trade reduced employment of workers with a high-school education or less by 6.8 percent and those with a college degree by 4.7 percent. In 1990 such changes were each less than 2 percent of the total number of such workers in the U.S. economy.

Conclusion

In summary, my analysis suggests that the impact of trade on the availability of high-rent opportunities for unskilled workers has been very small and cannot account for more than a trivial proportion of the high-school—college wage differential. The overall declines in rents have been small, and the effects on the availability of high-rent jobs have also been small, compared with the total number of workers in the labor force. At most, the effect appears to be about 0.2 or 0.3 percent. This is a far cry from the 1.3 points of the 13 percent differential that Borjas and Ramey found.

Why do these conclusions differ from those of Borjas and Ramey? In the first place, Borjas and Ramey assume *all* of the decline in the share of employment in durable goods is due to trade. They ignore the role of shifts in demand and increases in productivity growth. In fact, the effects of trade on the size of the durable goods sector was not very large between 1978 and 1990, since the United States already had a sizable trade deficit in durable manufactured goods in 1978. Indeed, after 1978 the rise in the manufacturing trade deficit was concentrated in nondurable goods. In the second place, the size of the average rents estimated by

Katz and Summers is somewhat lower than that assumed by Borjas and Ramey. And in the third place, Borjas and Ramey fail to account for the fact that, aside from primary metals, worker rents in highly concentrated industries have not eroded; indeed, there is no correlation between two-digit industry wage changes between 1978 and 1990 and estimates of industry rents.

Finally, it should be stressed that America's trade deficit in durable goods is heavily concentrated in its developed-country trade. The United States actually has a trade surplus with the developing countries in durable goods. Thus the issue of rent erosion as operating specifically through trade pressures is an argument mainly about U.S. trade with developed rather than with developing countries. Indeed, Borjas and Ramey do not find significant effects in their estimates of increases in import penetration in industries with low concentration ratios, which are those in which developing countries play a larger role.[11]

The conclusion that trade had only a small impact operating through shifting rents is corroborated by studies of the U.S. labor market as a whole. These find, for example, that a small share of the rising inequality can be explained by the decline in unionized sectors and the erosion of union rents. John Bound and George Johnson conclude that changes in the share of unionization explain just 1.3 percent of the 16.3 percent rise in the premium earned by male college graduates over high-school graduates in the 1980s.[12]

Appendix 4A. Literature Review of Relative Industry Wages and Employment

Several studies have estimated the impact of trade on relative industry wages. Some of these use sectoral trade balances (expressed as shares of domestic consumption) as an independent variable; others use measures of trade prices.[13] In these studies, however, results are often not signifi-

---

11. Oliveira-Martins (1994), for example, finds that the relative import share in imports from Asian newly industrializing countries in OECD imports is particularly large in industries that are not concentrated.

12. Bound and Johnson (1992, p. 379).

13. For example, Grossman (1987), Freeman and Katz (1991), and Lawrence and Lawrence (1985) examined the impact of trade on relative earnings in the United States; the OECD Jobs Study (1994), Larre (1995), Oliveira-Martins (1994), and Neven and Wyplosz (1994) explore these relationships internationally.

cant and in many cases increased trade is associated with relatively *higher* rather than lower levels of industry wages. Gene Grossman found a link between trade prices and industry wages in only two of the nine industries he examined.[14] Freeman and Katz find a small but statistically significant relationship between imports and wages as do Colin Lawrence and Robert Lawrence.[15] In the study by Benedicte Larre, which pools cross-sectional and time-series data from twelve countries, the most significant relationships between import competition in general and relative employment and wages were observed in high-skill industries, contrary to the belief that high-manual industries are more vulnerable to changes in trade competition. In several cases, particularly in Europe, however, increased import penetration was associated with *higher* rather than lower average compensation. Similarly, Damien Neven and Charles Wyplosz obtain diverse results. Reductions in import prices were associated with increases in wages and employment in twenty-eight cases, and decreases in fifty-three. Patrick Messerlin finds that in France wages of skilled workers move differently in export- and import-competing industries.[16]

There is also evidence in the literature that both labor- and product-market structures affect wage and employment responses. Noel Gaston and Daniel Trefler find in the United States that union wage premiums are sensitive to import competition, whereas nonunion premiums are not. David MacPherson and James Stewart conclude that a 10 percent rise in the share of imports lowered the union wage differential by 2 percent, although in general wages of both union and nonunion workers were far less sensitive to imports as the percentage organized increased.[17]

In his cross-national study of relative wages in twenty-two sectors across twelve OECD countries, Oliveira-Martins divides sectors into different categories on the basis of concentration and product differentiation. He finds that import penetration tends to reduce wages in industries with low product differentiation, whereas the relationship between import growth and average wages is positive in industries with high product

14. The OECD study did find that *employment* in a small number of labor-intensive industries (textiles, clothing, leather; office and computing machinery; radio-TV-communications) was reduced by trade, but with coefficients that were relatively small.

15. See also Orr and Orr (1984) for findings of wage responses in trade sensitive industries.

16. Messerlin (1995).

17. Gaston and Trefler (1992); MacPherson and Stewart (1990, p. 434).

differentiation. As regards the United States, James Galbraith and Paulo Du Pin Calmon find that in low-wage sectors competition from developing countries has strong disciplining effects, but it does not in high-wage sectors. They also find that relative wages in heavy industry are not depressed by import competition.[18]

One implication of Oliveira-Martins's results and those of others finding a positive association between wages and imports is that adjustment takes place in some sectors through relative employment changes rather than wage changes. A second implication may be that trade tends to displace low-paid (mainly manual) workers, thus affecting average wages through the shifting of the labor-force composition. A third is that the findings support a variant of a model laid out by Lawrence and Lawrence in 1985, in which increased import penetration is associated with higher rather than lower wages as unions engage in endgame bargaining and seek to extract rents.[19] A fourth implication, however, is reverse causation: that high wages lead to a loss in competitiveness and thus increased imports. To test this hypothesis, one would require a simultaneous-equations testing approach.

Indeed, Ana Ravenga ascribes negative findings such as these to a failure to correct the trade variable for endogeneity.[20] Applying two-stage least squares using instrumental variables techniques, she finds statistically significant effects linking import prices to industry employment and wages (positively), although she estimates the impact on wages to be much smaller than on employment. Import price elasticities range from 0.24 to 0.39 for employment and from 0.06 to 0.09 for wages. She concludes that "the relative size of these elasticities suggests that labor is quite mobile across industries—the impact on the return to labor of an adverse trade shock in a particular industry seems to be quite small."[21] In particular, she estimates that the very substantial appreciation of the

---

18. Oliveira-Martins (1994); Galbraith and Du Pin Calmon (1993).

19. In the Lawrence and Lawrence model, the union is a monopolist whose wage demand depends on the derived demand elasticity. Although import competition exerts downward pressure on relative wages by making final demand more elastic, it may also lower the demand elasticity by making additional investment in capital substitution less attractive. Lawrence and Lawrence argue that this effect is particularly important in capital-intensive industries such as steel. Grossman (1984) obtains similar results by modeling the median union member's responses to international competition.

20. Ravenga (1992).

21. Ravenga (1992, p. 257).

dollar between 1980 and 1985, which reduced import prices by 19 percent, lowered wages in the industries in her sample by about 2 percent, an amount that is noticeable but too small to provide much explanation for the large increase in the education premium in the United States in the 1980s.

CHAPTER FIVE

Multinationals and Outsourcing

OVER THE PAST decade global foreign direct investment has increased much more rapidly than trade. Attention has therefore been particularly focused on multinational corporations, which are seen as a conduit for technology from North to South and for components and other products in the reverse direction. In France a much publicized report by the then senator and now economics and finance minister Jean Arthuis describes an "alarming situation" in which delocalization (that is, the movement of production plants to low-cost locations abroad) is seen as a major contributor to the employment declines in such industries as electronics, textiles, clothing, and footwear.[1] Employment in those industries has been reduced by 50 percent in France over the past decade. The report is particularly harsh on Asian competitors, who are seen as competing through unfair strategies such as social dumping, undervalued currencies, and closed domestic markets.

As noted by the *World Investment Report* of 1994, however, critics have pointed out that the Arthuis report confused technological change and the impact of recession with that of foreign direct investment. The *World Investment Report* quotes a report by Madeuf which finds that less than 5 percent of the total outward stock of foreign direct investment held by French multinationals represents delocalization in the strict sense of the

1. Arthuis (1993).

89

word; that is, plants that closed and relocated abroad.[2] Similarly, Patrick Messerlin concludes that both inward and outward French capital flows were small in relation to domestic gross investment even in sectors where employment was declining.[3]

The UN Conference on Trade and Development estimates that in 1992, 73 million persons were employed in multinationals or their affiliates, with U.S. multinationals accounting for 25 million.[4] Of this total, as reported in table 5-1, however, only 29 million persons worked in foreign affiliates and 12 million in developing countries, with 3 million in China alone. Since multinational employment continues to constitute a negligible share of the world's labor force—about 3 percent—this suggests, as Richard Freeman points out, that the direct transfer of technology to developing countries through the operations of multinationals remains small.[5]

Table 5-1 also reports employment in the foreign manufacturing affiliates of multinationals of major home countries. Interestingly, foreign multinational employment is fairly large compared with domestic manufacturing employment in two countries in which particular concern has been expressed about runaway plants: in France (31 percent) and in the United States (23 percent). Employment in these countries' overseas manufacturing affiliates located in developing countries was 14 percent and 12 percent of their domestic manufacturing employment, respectively. This might explain why concerns about the overseas activities of multinationals have become particularly prominent in these two countries. It is striking, however, particularly given the concerns raised in France about Asia, that French multinational employment in Asian affiliates accounts for less than a quarter of French multinational employment in their foreign affiliates in developing countries.

As reported in table 5-2, U.S. firms with foreign operations did not contribute to employment growth within the United States from 1977 to 1989—a remarkable result, given the rise of about 30 percent in U.S. employment over that period.[6] These firms are particularly important in the U.S. manufacturing sector; indeed, they account for more than half

2. UNCTAD (1994).
3. Messerlin (1995).
4. UNCTAD (1994).
5. Freeman (forthcoming).
6. In 1989 total nonbank multinational employment in the United States was 18.8 million, about the same as the 18.9 million in 1977.

Table 5-1. *Employment in Foreign Manufacturing Affiliates, by Host Region, Selected Developed Home Countries, 1990, 1991, 1992*[a]

Thousands

Item	France (1992)	Germany (1991)	Italy (1991)	Japan (1990)	Sweden (1990)	Switzerland (1990)	United States (1991)
Developed countries	1,634	1,774	322	767	268	833	4,760
European Union	1,031	834	251	209	71	482	2,768
Developing countries	632	601	168	814	42	215	2,138
Latin America	195	361	97	115	n.a.	n.a.	n.a.
Asia	134	188	26	678	11	88	710
Total	2,268	2,375	511	1,550	308	1,048	6,898
Manufacturing	1,359	1,660	511	1,261	n.a.	837	4,270
Domestic manufacturing employment	4,367	9,080	5,028	15,348	935	n.a.	18,428
Ratio of developing country employment to domestic manufacturing	0.14	0.07	0.03	0.05	0.04	n.a.	0.12
Ratio of affiliate to domestic manufacturing employment	0.31	0.18	0.10	0.08	n.a.	n.a.	0.23

Sources: UNCTAD (1994); OECD STAN database.

n.a.: Not available.

a. In 1985 there were 15 million affiliates in developed countries; in 1990, 17 million; in 1992, 17 million. In 1985 there were 7 million affiliates in developing countries; in 1990, 9 million; in 1992, 12 million. In 1990 there were 3 million affiliates in China; in 1992, 6 million.

Table 5-2. *Employment in U.S. Multinationals, 1977–89*

| | Employment figures (thousands) | | | | | | | | | Employment ratios: production workers/ nonproduction workers | | | Compensation ratios: production workers/ nonproduction workers | | |
| | Total | | | Production workers | | | Nonproduction workers | | | | | | | | |
Item	1977	1989	Percent change	1977	1989	Percent change	1977	1989	Percent change	1977	1989	Percent change	1977	1989	Percent change
United States[a]															
Total[b]	67,344	90,644	34.6	55,179	73,474	33.2	12,165	17,170	41.1	4.54	4.28	-5.7	[c]	0.66	-6.8
Manufacturing	19,682	19,426	-1.3	14,135	13,257	-6.2	5,547	6,169	11.2	2.55	2.15	-15.7	n.a.	n.a.	n.a.
Multinationals[d]															
Total	18,885	18,765	-0.6	n.a.	n.a.	n.a.	n.a.	n.a.	n.a.	n.a.	n.a.	n.a.	n.a.	n.a.	n.a.
Manufacturing	11,775	10,127	-14.0	7,257	n.a.	n.a.	4,518	n.a.	n.a.	1.61	n.a.	n.a.	0.78	n.a.	n.a.
Majority-owned manufacturing foreign affiliates[e]															
In developed countries	2,754	2,167	-21.3	1,695	1,196	-29.5	1,059	971	-8.3	1.60	1.23	-23.1	0.75	0.66	-10.8
Canada	562	455	-19.2	358	274	-23.5	204	181	-11.5	1.76	1.52	-13.6	0.86	0.81	-5.2
Europe	1,951	1,509	-22.6	1,202	828	-31.1	749	681	-9.1	1.60	1.22	-24.2	0.70	0.63	-10.0
Japan	40	75	86.6	14	23	62.0	26	52	99.7	0.53	0.43	-18.9	0.75	0.69	-8.5
Australia, New Zealand, South Africa	201	129	-35.8	122	71	-41.3	80	58	-27.4	1.53	1.23	-19.1	0.78	0.68	-12.5
In developing countries	1,019	1,079	5.9	675	679	0.6	344	400	16.4	1.96	1.70	-13.6	0.47	0.41	-12.8
Total	3,773	3,247	-14.0	2,371	1,875	-20.9	1,403	1,371	-2.2	1.69	1.37	-19.1	0.68	0.59	-14.2

In industries

Food and kindred products	377	308	−18.5	248	184	−25.9	129	124	−4.2	1.93	1.49	−22.7	0.57	0.62	9.8
Textile products and apparel	102	82	−19.5	80	59	−27.2	21	23	9.3	3.78	2.52	−33.3	0.47	0.59	23.7
Chemicals and allied products	464	475	2.2	233	227	−2.5	231	247	6.9	1.01	0.92	−8.8	0.71	0.64	−9.1
Primary and fabricated metals	229	179	−21.9	158	117	−26.1	71	62	−12.5	2.23	1.88	−15.6	0.80	0.73	−9.4
Machinery, except electrical	523	508	−2.9	270	254	−6.0	253	254	0.4	1.07	1.00	−6.4	0.61	0.59	−3.9
Electric and electronic equipment	629	455	−27.7	422	288	−31.8	207	167	−19.3	2.03	1.72	−15.5	0.56	0.54	−4.3
Transportation equipment	740	597	−19.4	507	365	−28.0	233	231	−0.9	2.17	1.58	−27.3	0.97	0.61	−37.2
Other manufacturing	709	645	−9.0	452	382	−15.5	257	263	2.3	1.76	1.45	−17.4	0.75	0.59	−21.0
Total	3,773	3,247	−14.0	2,371	1,875	−20.9	1,403	1,371	−2.2	1.69	1.37	−19.1	0.68	0.59	−14.2

n.a. Not available.

a. Labor force totals according to the U.S. Department of Labor, *Employment, Hours, and Earnings, United States, 1909–90*, vol. 1, 1991.

b. Figures for private nonfarm establishments. The total nonfarm figures are 1977 - $82.471 million; 1989 - $108.413 million.

c. The compensation ratio for total U.S. employment is a comparison of the white-collar–blue-collar cost indexes in 1977 and 1989, as published by the U.S. Bureau of Labor Statistics.

d. According to and based on U.S. Department of Commerce, *U.S. Direct Investment Abroad, 1977; U.S. Direct Investment Abroad, 1989.* Information is for nonbank U.S. parents of nonbank U.S. affiliates.

e. Classified by industry of affiliate. According to the Department of Commerce publications listed in note d.

of all manufacturing employment. However, between 1977 and 1989 their manufacturing employment in the United States fell 14 percent, considerably faster than the drop of 1.2 percent in total manufacturing employment over the same period. Similarly, between 1989 and 1993 employment in multinational manufacturing parents fell by almost 9 percent, compared with a 7.2 percent drop in U.S. manufacturing employment as a whole.[7]

This sluggish employment growth in U.S. multinationals has been attributed by many Americans to the impact of their foreign operations. It is widely perceived in the United States that many of the jobs in those firms have moved abroad. Drawn by low labor costs and low labor standards, multinational corporations are seen as having relocated their production toward low-wage countries. In particular, the jobs of blue-collar workers are viewed as vulnerable to this development. Such international outsourcing could, in principle, provide an alternative explanation of the widespread decline *both* in relative blue-collar wages and in the ratio of blue- to white-collar workers employed in U.S. manufacturing.

If outsourcing is important, the decline in blue-collar intensity in the United States should be associated with an increase in blue-collar intensity abroad. In addition, in line with the Stolper-Samuelson theorem, if developing countries lower their trade barriers and increase their specialization in unskilled-labor-intensive products, in developing countries the relative wages of production workers should rise, while in developed countries they should fall. Also, one might expect to see an important increase in the share of sales by foreign affiliates going to the United States. On the other hand, if global changes in technology were dominant, one should see *parallel* increases in the ratio of blue- to white-collar employment in the United States and the rest of the world as well as similar movements in wages.

Employment and compensation data for U.S. multinationals in 1977 and 1989 are shown in table 5-2. Several features are noteworthy. In 1989 U.S. manufacturing multinationals employed more than 13 million people, about a quarter of whom were in their foreign affiliates. The data

7. The data on U.S. multinational activity were collected in extensive and comprehensive benchmark surveys by the U.S. Bureau of Economic Analysis in 1977 and 1989. These data provide an unusually comprehensive view of developments worldwide among an important group of actors. The data should, however, be treated with care, particularly because the aggregate level at which I report them here could conceal important compositional changes by country and industry. Further, all activities of each firm are ascribed to a single industry, which could lead to misclassification of some activity.

suggest that, overall, multinationals are not necessarily attracted abroad simply by cheap labor; indeed, only about a third of U.S. multinationals' affiliate manufacturing employment is in developing countries. Nonetheless, within developing countries, multinationals do use production workers more intensively than in developed countries and, on average, production workers are paid about half rather than three-quarters the compensation of nonproduction workers. It is noteworthy that the ratio of production to nonproduction workers in developing countries of 1.7 in 1989 was similar to the ratios in Europe and Canada of 1.6 and 1.8, respectively, in 1977.

Consider, now, changes in the data between 1977 and 1989 (table 5-2). These do not support the common perception that overseas employment in U.S.-owned manufacturing foreign affiliates has increased. Indeed, employment in the majority-U.S.-owned foreign manufacturing affiliates of U.S. multinationals declined by 14 percent, a decline similar to that experienced in their U.S. parents. This decline was mainly due to shrinkage in the European operations of U.S. multinationals, where total employment fell by 23 percent and production worker employment plunged by 31 percent. Employment grew by about 6 percent between 1977 and 1989 in U.S. manufacturing multinationals in developing countries. But the magnitude of employment in these U.S. foreign affiliates is relatively small. The aggregate rise in employment was just 60,000. This employment growth is small when compared with the drop of 1.7 million in employment that occurred in U.S. manufacturing parents over the same period and the 500,000 drop in manufacturing foreign affiliates over the same period. The overall share of developing countries in the employment of U.S. majority-owned foreign manufacturing affiliates increased from 27 to 34 percent, and their share in the worldwide employment of manufacturing multinationals (that is, in both U.S. parents and foreign affiliates) increased from 6.8 to 8.1 percent.[8]

What about production-worker employment in these affiliates? Of the 60,000-person growth in all employment, only 4,000 were production

8. More recent data, which reflect the relatively earlier occurrence of recession in the United States, show that overseas employment in U.S. multinationals was more robust than in U.S. parents. Between 1989 and 1991 U.S.-based employment in multinational parents declined by 5.1 percent (987,000). By contrast, employment in majority-owned manufacturing affiliates increased by 50,700, or 1.6 percent. It would be erroneous to assume a causal connection between these developments, but even if one were to make such a connection, less than 10 percent of U.S. employment loss could be accounted for jobs that were transferred abroad.

workers. As estimated by Matthew Slaughter, declines in production-worker employment occurred in Europe (− 370,700), Central and South America, excluding Mexico (− 75,300). In Mexico production-worker employment increased by 80,900. In Asian countries, though increases were recorded, they were surprisingly small: Malaysia (15,600), Singapore (10,400), South Korea (3,900), and Thailand (11,700).[9] There is, therefore, little evidence that, on balance, large numbers of production-worker jobs are shifting within U.S. multinationals away from the United States toward the developing countries.

The ratio of production to nonproduction workers employed in U.S. manufacturing operations worldwide has fallen precipitously. Indeed, the declines are of similar magnitude in U.S. manufacturing parents (− 15.7 percent) and in their affiliates in developing countries (− 13.6 per cent). The declines were particularly large in Europe (− 24.2 percent) and in Australia, South Africa, and New Zealand (− 19.1 percent). Only in Mexico did the ratio increase. There were also declines in this ratio in most major industries. According to Slaughter, who estimated these changes at a three-digit level, three industries were exceptional and did experience both rising foreign employment in production workers and falling ratios of nonproduction to production workers. These were tobacco products (+ 4,000 and − 15.7 percent), a subset of chemical products (SIC 285, 288, and 289) (+ 10,900 and − 25.4 percent), and computers and office equipment (+ 37,500 and − 27.4 percent).[10]

As I noted earlier, if the Stolper-Samuelson story were dominant, one would expect to see the relative wages of production workers moving in opposite directions in developed and developing countries. Instead, what one sees is that relative wages of production workers have fallen worldwide. *Together, the picture that emerges appears far more consistent with a common shift in technology and organizational structures than with expanding trade as the explanation. Worldwide, one sees a rise in the relative employment of nonproduction workers despite the increase in their relative wage.*[11]

9. Slaughter (1993, p. 23).

10. Slaughter (1993, p. 24).

11. Davis (1992) finds that increased trade is associated with an international convergence across several countries of relative-wage structures. He concludes that the factor-price-equalization effect has been more than offset by the growing divergence across countries of relative industry wage structures.

Robert Feenstra and Gordon Hanson call these conclusions into question in the context of a model that departs from the traditional Hecksher-Ohlin-Samuelson framework by assuming complete specialization.[12] In their framework both the North and the South produce components that are in turn used to produce a single world product. The components can be ranked along a continuum, and there is no factor-price equalization. Instead, skilled labor is relatively cheap in the North and unskilled labor is relatively cheap in the South. Accordingly, the North produces the more skill-intensive components. As the South grows, however, activities are transferred to the South. These are the least skill-intensive activities in the North but become the highest in the South. The effect is reminiscent of the joke (told by MIT faculty) about the professor who moved from MIT to Harvard and raised the average IQ in both places. The result is that in both the North and South the demand for skilled workers increases and so does their relative wage.

This model offers a plausible alternative to that of global technological change. It would explain precisely the configuration of changes that are detailed in table 5-2: higher ratios of nonproduction to production workers in both the United States and the developing countries and higher relative wages for nonproduction workers in both countries. Feenstra and Hansen also note that a corollary of their theory is that prices of products produced in the North (which are more skill intensive) rise relative to the products produced in the South. Indeed, as support for their theory, they cite the data reported in chapter 3 for the United States, Germany, and Japan, which show smaller rises in import prices than those for domestic goods. However, they ignore a more direct test of their theory: its implication that the terms of trade of the developed countries should improve. There is only weak support for this in the case of the United States, where the terms of trade for manufactured goods remained constant over the 1980s.[13] Moreover, the theory implies that average real wages in the North should rise more rapidly than output per worker, a development that clearly did not occur in the 1980s, as the discussion in chapter 1 makes clear.

Finally, in the theory put forward by Feenstra and Hanson, the rise in the ratio of skilled to unskilled workers in the developing countries results

12. Feenstra and Hanson (1994).
13. Lawrence (1990).

from a change in the industry mix of employment rather than within-industry shifts. If Feenstra and Hanson are correct, therefore, one should find particularly rapid employment growth in developing-country foreign affiliates in industries with relatively high ratios of nonproduction workers. However, on the basis of a shift-share analysis, I conclude that this does not appear to have occurred. The expansion in employment in developing-country foreign affiliates of U.S. companies was not related to their initial skill intensities; instead, the increased use of skilled workers occurred within industries.

An alternative interpretation of the rising ratio of nonproduction to production workers in U.S. manufacturing in the 1980s is that it represents increased foreign outsourcing. Indeed, if the production of labor-intensive activities were moved abroad, that, rather than a change in technology, could explain the rise in the ratio of nonproduction to production workers found in U.S. manufacturing. If this were true, one would expect to find smaller shifts within industries. However, in Lawrence and Slaughter we found the shifts as pervasive at the four-digit SIC level as at the three-digit level.[14] Moreover, Eli Berman, John Bound, and Zvi Griliches note that according to the 1987 census of manufacturing very little of materials outsourced came from the same SIC three-digit industry as the establishment itself.[15]

Fortunately, there are data on imported products purchased by U.S. multinational parents. Figure 5-1 gives a picture of the quantitative importance of various forms of outsourcing. As might be expected for a period in which the U.S. trade deficit increased, between 1982 and 1989 there was a rapid increase in the purchases of manufactured goods by U.S.-based multinationals from their foreign affiliates: from $25 billion in 1982 to $61.2 billion in 1989. Purchases from unaffiliated foreigners increased even more rapidly, from $16.1 to $45.3 billion. Although the increase was rapid, these imports still represent only a small share of the

---

14. Lawrence and Slaughter (1993).

15. Berman, Bound, and Griliches (1992). Feenstra and Hanson (1994) raise questions about the findings of Berman, Bound, and Griliches because they note materials can be resold several times and counted as imports only once. They also object that imports of finished products that are sold (often with U.S. brand names) without added value are unlikely to be counted as materials. Machin (1994) examines establishment-level data from the United Kingdom and finds that most of the rise in the share of nonmanuals within total employment occurred within establishments, particularly in increased relative employment of middle managers and senior professionals. Moreover, these shifts were found to be largest in more R&D-intensive industries and in establishments that introduced microcomputers.

Figure 5-1. *Sourcing Comparison for U.S. Manufacturing Multinationals and Their Majority-Owned Affiliates*

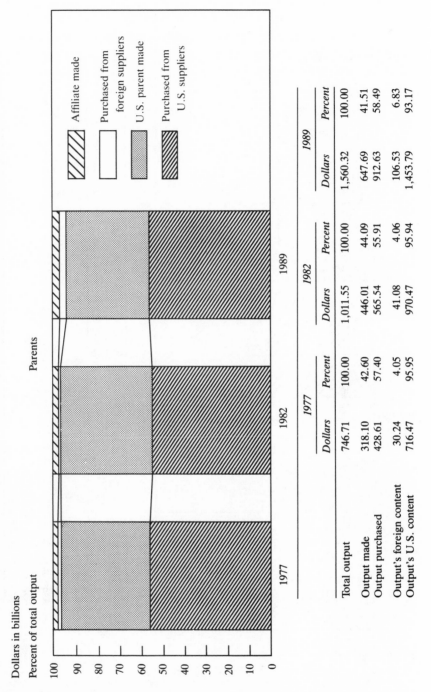

	1977		1982		1989	
	Dollars	*Percent*	*Dollars*	*Percent*	*Dollars*	*Percent*
Total output	746.71	100.00	1,011.55	100.00	1,560.32	100.00
Output made	318.10	42.60	446.01	44.09	647.69	41.51
Output purchased	428.61	57.40	565.54	55.91	912.63	58.49
Output's foreign content	30.24	4.05	41.08	4.06	106.53	6.83
Output's U.S. content	716.47	95.95	970.47	95.94	1,453.79	93.17

Figure 5-1 *(continued)*

Percent total output

Majority-owned manufacturing affiliates

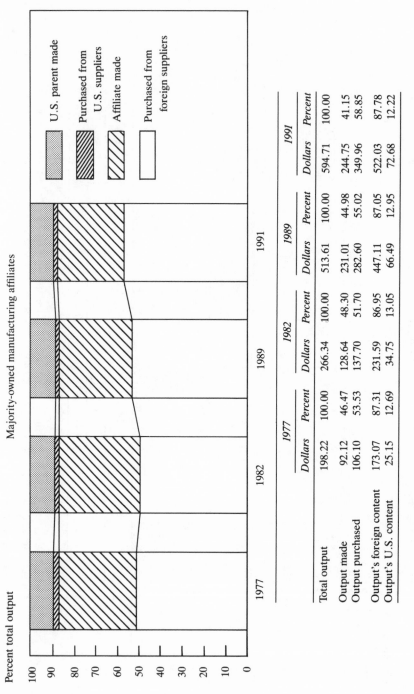

	1977		1982		1989		1991	
	Dollars	*Percent*	*Dollars*	*Percent*	*Dollars*	*Percent*	*Dollars*	*Percent*
Total output	198.22	100.00	266.34	100.00	513.61	100.00	594.71	100.00
Output made	92.12	46.47	128.64	48.30	231.01	44.98	244.75	41.15
Output purchased	106.10	53.53	137.70	51.70	282.60	55.02	349.96	58.85
Output's foreign content	173.07	87.31	231.59	86.95	447.11	87.05	522.03	87.78
Output's U.S. content	25.15	12.69	34.75	13.05	66.49	12.95	72.68	12.22

Legend: U.S. parent made; Purchased from U.S. suppliers; Affiliate made; Purchased from foreign suppliers.

Source: Based on information provided by the Department of Commerce's Bureau of Economic Analysis—Survey of Current Business, February 1994.

total sales of U.S. multinational parents, rising from 4.1 percent in 1982 to 6.8 percent in 1989.[16] Moreover, these numbers refer to purchases from both developed and developing countries.[17] Manufactured imports from *developing* countries were roughly a third of these shares. These imports are thus too small to have employment and wage shifts of the size they are alleged to have.[18]

There is interesting evidence that large U.S. firms are downsizing, slimming down to the core activities that are essential to their operations; less vital activities are performed in smaller and more flexible suppliers. Overall value-added within U.S. multinational parents fell from 41.6 percent of sales in 1982 to 37.6 percent in 1989. Of this 4.0 shift, almost 1.2 points represented a rise in domestic outsourcing and the remainder outsourcing from abroad. The slimming down that is evident in U.S. parents is even more striking in the behavior of their foreign manufacturing affiliates. Between 1982 and 1989 value-added within these operations declined from 37.5 to 33.7 percent of sales, of which almost all represented a rise in inputs sourced abroad rather than in the United States. The data for 1991 suggest that this trend has continued, with the share of value-added performed in-house in affiliates declining to 30.6 percent. The share of inputs sourced by foreign affiliates from their U.S. parents and other U.S. sources remained fairly constant over this period.[19]

In sum, although there has been much discussion of globalization, this chapter brings out the fact that productivity levels of multinationals and their foreign subsidiaries in developing countries remain distinctly different. The evidence drawn from data on U.S. multinationals points to the dominant impact of a commonly shared technological and organizational change rather than the impact of trade and international outsourcing.

16. Gross product in U.S. manufacturing was $647 billion in 1982 and $1,004.6 billion in 1989.

17. Sales of U.S. foreign affiliates of manufactured goods from developing countries to all U.S. purchasers increased from $7.5 billion in 1982 to about $20 billion in 1989.

18. The Bureau of Economic Analysis reaches similar conclusions. In the *Survey of Current Business*, July 1993, the BEA compared employment patterns in high- and low-wage countries over the period 1982 to 1991. The low-wage share of MOFA employment increased by 3 percentage points, to 34 percent. Between 1982 and 1989 the BEA finds that the domestic content of U.S. parents' output in manufacturing decreased from 96 to 93 percent.

19. Slaughter (1993) produces evidence that foreign labor and U.S. labor are price complements rather than substitutes. A 1 percent drop in foreign wages tends to raise home employment by nearly 0.1 percent.

Employment fell both in U.S. parents and in affiliates in developed countries and grew only modestly in developing countries. In foreign affiliates in both developed and developing countries, the relative compensation of nonproduction workers increased, and the ratio of production to nonproduction workers fell. Although U.S. parent sourcing from overseas affiliates grew rapidly, the increase accounted for only a small share of total sales.

There is a widespread view that since both technology and capital are increasingly mobile, productivity is as high in U.S. multinationals abroad as in the United States. If that is true, one might expect to see lower wages per worker but similar levels of output per worker. But, as reported in table 5-3, measured in current U.S. dollars, output per employee in developing countries in 1989 was about 40 percent of output per employee in developed countries. By contrast, compensation per employee averaged 29 percent of developed-country levels. (Production workers received 23 percent of the compensation of their developed-country counterparts; nonproduction workers received 37 percent, while nonwage income per worker was 49.7 percent of developed-country levels.)

Conclusion

Globalization is increasingly spoken of as the dominant source of structural change in the OECD with the multinational corporation as its major agent. There is a widespread perception that as options to relocate abroad increase and corporations become increasingly mobile, labor the immobile factor, labor, the immobile factor, bears more of the costs. However, these effects do not seem to be large.

In the previous chapters I showed that in the United States wage premiums for high-school workers in concentrated industries have not declined significantly. In this chapter I add evidence that declining employment, increasing skill intensity, and rising skill premiums are widespread both in multinational headquarters and in foreign affiliates in developed and developing countries—with the exception of Mexico. Moreover, labor productivity appears much higher in developed than in developing affiliates, suggesting that claims of similar technological capabilities are inaccurate. This common shift toward increasing skill in-

Table 5-3. *Output and Employment in U.S. Manufacturing Foreign Affiliates, 1989*

Item	Output (millions of 1989 dollars)	Number of employees	Compensation per worker	1989 dollars Net income per worker	1989 dollars Output per worker
Developed countries					
All workers	143,244	2,167,300	33,028	12,587	66,093
Production workers	n.a.	1,196,100	26,943	n.a.	n.a.
Nonproduction workers	n.a.	971,200	40,523	n.a.	n.a.
Developing countries					
All workers	28,764	1,079,400	9,404	6,250	26,648
Production workers	n.a.	679,200	6,110	n.a.	n.a.
Nonproduction workers	n.a.	400,200	14,955	n.a.	n.a.
Addenda: Ratio of developing to developed countries					
Compensation per worker					
All		0.28			
Production		0.23			
Nonproduction		0.37			
Gross product per worker		0.40			
Net income per worker		0.50			

Sources: U.S. Department of Commerce, *U.S. Direct Investment Abroad, 1989, Benchmark Survey; Survey of Current Business,* February 1994.

tensity globally is strongly suggestive of a technological shock rather than the massive relocation of unskilled labor-intensive operations to developing countries. Despite the increasing attention paid to globalization, therefore, there is considerable evidence pointing to important roles for domestic and technological factors in labor market performance.

CHAPTER SIX

The Future

DEVELOPING COUNTRIES throughout the world are increasing their trade at a dramatic pace. For example, China, the world's largest developing economy has also been the economy growing most rapidly. In 1994 China was already the world's third largest economy, and within a decade it is expected to be the second largest. Between 1980 and 1993 Chinese export volumes increased at the very rapid pace of 13 percent annually. Yet in the context of other dynamic Asian economies, the growth of China's exports was not exceptional; several countries have sustained a growth in export volume of about 10 percent for a decade or more. By contrast, the growth prospects for developed countries are much more modest. Typical estimates of potential growth in the developed world for the next decade are in the range of 2.5 percent.

If large, and potentially large, economies like India, China, and Indonesia grow rapidly, the question of future effects of such trade on OECD labor markets looms large. Almost all the recent studies of the links between trade and wages have looked backward. But the relationship between trade and wages could be even more relevant in the coming decades. Whatever economists may believe about the past, many fear a future in which the wages of the unskilled in developed countries are driven down to those of their unskilled counterparts in developing countries. Indeed, this is the specter of factor-price equalization that haunts many conversations about such trade.

In what follows, I present evidence which suggests that although growing international trade could lead to lower relative and real wages for unskilled workers, the fears of large wage losses appear misplaced. In

105

general, this process will bring benefits to the OECD as a whole. Over the next fifteen years an expansion in trade between the OECD and the developing countries at the double-digit pace of the past decade would bring about a major change in the structure of tradable-goods production in the OECD. In particular, the OECD could see a decline in large segments of its basic industrial activities as these are replaced by imports from emerging markets. Matching this decline, however, will be an expansion of skill-intensive activities that will provide an offsetting source of growth.

Why does the process of factor-price equalization not occur? In a single world market, to remain in production, firms must be able to match the costs of their competitors. If none have a technological advantage, they will all be able to afford to pay only the same wages and capital costs. Thus the factor-price equalization theorem in conventional trade theory predicts that, given similar technologies, *if countries produce similar products*, they will also have similar wage rates (and other factor prices). In this world, trade serves as a substitute for factor mobility. Just as free immigration would equalize wage rates, so too would free trade. Another remarkable feature of such a world is that as long as countries produce enough products in common their factor prices will be equalized, regardless of the share of trade or tradable goods in their overall production.[1]

A key aspect of such a world is that countries produce similar products. Once countries become fully specialized, the strong links between international wages and product prices break down. For example, if a country has no domestic production of clothing, imports of clothing will no longer directly affect wages. One way for workers in developed economies to avoid head-to-head competition with workers in developing countries, therefore, is to specialize in producing products that developing countries do not produce. Under these conditions, wages and other factor prices in the developed countries will be determined only by the derived demands for the goods and services that they actually produce; namely, those that are exported and those that are not traded. Put simply, the floor on the wages of unskilled workers in the OECD is not what workers earn in the textile industries of China and India but what they can earn if they are all employed in export and domestic industries in the

---

1. This point has particularly been stressed by Leamer (forthcoming).

OECD. In the presence of full specialization, therefore, free trade does not have the same impact on wages as free immigration.[2]

Where might this floor lie? In what follows, I construct a scenario using data from the United States in 1990 to explore the implications of a very large expansion in U.S. manufactured-goods trade with developing countries. I consider the impact on U.S. labor of moving to complete specialization, in which industries that compete with manufactured imports from developing countries are totally eliminated.

High-Skill and Basic Industries

How might such import-competing industries be defined? I am interested not necessarily in a serious prediction but in one that all would agree presents an extreme case. In table 6-1, I report data on U.S. two-digit SIC industries ranked according to the share of full-time workers with a high-school education or less—high-school workers—in the labor force in 1990.[3] The industries are listed in ascending order. They range from tobacco, in which high-school workers accounted for just 43 percent of employment, to apparel, in which they constituted 85 percent. The industries fall into two distinct groups. There is one group of seven industries in which high-school employment shares range from 43 to 53 percent and a second group with shares ranging between 65 and 85 percent. There are no two-digit industries between 53 and 65 percent. The first group, which I define as high-skill industries, includes printing and tobacco plus the industries that are usually classified as high-tech, namely chemicals, machinery, and instruments. The second group, which I define as basic, includes all other industries.

Clearly, given the level of aggregation, this is a fairly crude approximation, but it does have strong predictive value with respect to trade with developing countries. In 1990 the high-skill industries accounted for about three-quarters of all U.S. manufactured exports to developing countries, while the basic industries accounted for almost 60 percent of U.S. manufactured imports from developing countries. Moreover, exports to developing countries count for much higher shares of value-added

2. Deardorff and Courant (1989) have shown that the larger the share of nontraded goods, the quicker a country becomes fully specialized.

3. Industry SIC 29, petroleum refining, has been excluded.

Table 6-1. *Trade and Employment Characteristics of U.S. Manufacturing Industries, 1990*[a]

Standard industrial classification	HS/EMP	LDCEXP/ VA	LDCIMP/ VA	Share of LDCEXP	Share of LDCIMP	Share of MAN employment	Share of MAN VA	HS/COL wages	HS/ COL earnings
21. Tobacco	0.43	0.06	0.00	0.01	0.00	0.00	0.02	0.70	0.35
38. Instruments	0.45	0.10	0.06	0.05	0.02	0.04	0.04	0.56	0.31
28. Chemicals	0.46	0.10	0.02	0.14	0.02	0.07	0.12	0.62	0.35
27. Printing	0.49	0.00	0.01	0.00	0.00	0.08	0.08	0.73	0.42
35. Nonelectric machinery	0.50	0.16	0.12	0.19	0.11	0.12	0.10	0.64	0.39
36. Electrical machinery	0.50	0.14	0.20	0.18	0.20	0.10	0.11	0.55	0.35
37. Transportation equipment	0.53	0.13	0.06	0.17	0.06	0.13	0.11	0.67	0.43
Total high skill	0.50	0.11	0.08	0.74	0.42	0.54	0.57	0.63	0.39
26. Paper products	0.65	0.06	0.02	0.03	0.01	0.04	0.05	0.67	0.55
39. Miscellaneous manufacturing	0.67	0.07	0.60	0.01	0.09	0.02	0.02	0.62	0.55
30. Rubber	0.67	0.04	0.09	0.02	0.03	0.04	0.04	0.67	0.58
32. Stone, clay, and glass	0.68	0.03	0.06	0.01	0.02	0.03	0.03	0.64	0.58
34. Metal products	0.69	0.05	0.05	0.03	0.03	0.06	0.06	0.67	0.59
20. Food	0.71	0.05	0.05	0.06	0.05	0.09	0.11	0.66	0.62
33. Primary metals	0.73	0.08	0.16	0.04	0.06	0.04	0.04	0.72	0.67
25. Furniture	0.80	0.02	0.12	0.00	0.02	0.03	0.02	0.69	0.73
24. Lumber	0.81	0.05	0.06	0.01	0.01	0.03	0.02	0.67	0.74
31. Leather	0.81	0.15	2.01	0.01	0.07	0.01	0.00	0.57	0.71
22. Textiles	0.82	0.06	0.16	0.01	0.03	0.03	0.02	0.64	0.74
23. Apparel	0.85	0.05	0.68	0.02	0.16	0.05	0.03	0.54	0.75
Total basic	0.73	0.05	0.15	0.26	0.58	0.46	0.43	0.63	0.64

Sources: NBER Database; Sachs and Shatz estimates; CPS tapes.

a. HS/EMP = share of full-time employment with high-school degree or less in 1990; LDCEXP = U.S. exports of manufactured goods to developing countries; VA = value-added; LDCIMP = U.S. imports of manufactured goods from developing countries in 1990; MAN = manufacturing; COL = Full-time workers with some college education.

in the high-skill industries (11 percent) than in the basic industries (5 percent). On the other hand, the ratio of manufactured imports to domestic value-added is much higher for low-skill (15 percent) than for high-skill (8 percent), industries.

Several other features are noteworthy. On average, high-skill industries are larger than basic industries. Employment in each category accounted for roughly half of total manufacturing employment in 1990. Thus if the industries had simply been ranked according to the share of high-school employment and divided into two, the classification would have been the same. Value-added per worker, which averaged $73,000, was 14 percent higher in the high-skill group, so that this group accounted for a relatively higher share of total value-added in manufacturing (57 percent) than in employment (54 percent). Finally, the average share of high-school employment in the high-skill industries (50 percent) is in line with the share of high-school employment in the economy as a whole (49 percent) and not much higher than in the nonmanufacturing economy (46 percent).

An Illustrative Future Scenario

As reported in table 6-2, the United States completely replaces with imports from developing countries the 1990 domestic value-added of $552 billion that was produced in these basic industries. In turn, production and exports of the high-skill industries expand by an additional $552 billion in proportion to their 1990 output shares. As seen in the table, given constant ratios of inputs to outputs, this switch would eliminate the demand for the 8.7 million workers employed in basic industries (6.4 million high-school workers and 2.3 million college workers.) On the other hand, the increase in value-added of the high-skill manufacturing sector by $552 billion would raise demand for 7.6 million workers split evenly between high-school and college workers. All told, therefore, this substitution results in an excess supply of 2.6 million high-school workers and an excess demand for 1.5 million college workers. Thus given this alternative production structure for manufacturing and the same production and employment structure as prevailed in 1990 outside manufacturing, the desired economywide employment ratio of high-school to college workers is 88.2 percent. In fact, in 1990 the actual ratio demanded (and supplied) was 95.4 percent. *Thus, as compared with 1990, the relative demand for high-school workers would decline by 7.5 percent.* To clear

Table 6-2. A Future Scenario in Which the United States Fully Specializes in High-Skill Products

Item	High skill	Basic	Manufacturing	Nonmanufacturing	U.S. economy
			1990 Actual		
1. Value-added (billions)	742.05	552.45	1,294.5	n.a.	n.a.
2. Employment (millions)	10.18	8.68	18.86	86.17	105.03
3. Value-added/emp. (thousands)	72.89	63.65	68.64	n.a.	n.a.
4. High school emp. (million)	5.08	6.36	11.44	39.85	51.29
5. College emp. (million)	5.10	2.32	7.42	46.32	53.74
6. Share HS/emp (4)/(2)	0.50	0.73	0.61	0.46	0.49
7. Ratio HS/COL (4)/(5)	1.00	2.74	1.54	0.86	0.95
			Hypothetical		
8. Value-added (billions)	1,294.50	0.00	1,294.50	n.a.	n.a.
9. Employment (8)/(3)	17.76	0.00	17.76	n.a.	n.a.
10. High school (6) × (9)	8.86	0.00	8.86	39.85	48.71
11. College	8.90	0.00	8.90	46.32	55.22
12. Ratio HS/COL (10)/(11)	1.00	...	1.00	0.86	0.88
			Hypothetical to Actual		
13. Employment	7.58	-8.68	-1.10	n.a.	n.a.
14. High school	3.78	-6.36	-2.58	0.00	-2.58
15. College	3.80	-2.32	1.48	0.00	1.48
16. Ratio HS/COL	0.00	...	-0.55	...	-0.072
17. Percentage change in ratio of HS/COL					**-7.58**

Source: Author's calculations. See table 6-1.
n.a. Not available.

the labor market, therefore, the relative wage of high-school workers would have to fall to encourage firms in both high-skill manufacturing and the nonmanufacturing economy to change their demands. With lower wages for high-school workers, more would be employed in both sectors. If the elasticity of substitution between these types of labor is unity, that would require a decline in the *relative* high-school wage of 7.5 percent.

This is clearly a dramatic scenario. In 1990 U.S. imports from developing countries of manufactured goods amounted to $140 billion. In the alternative scenario they are assumed to increase by $550 billion, to $690 billion—in other words, there is a fivefold increase. If this increase took place over a fifteen-year period, it would correspond to an annual growth rate of 11.3 percent. These effects would build up over time and become larger in later years when trade volumes were larger. After ten years, only about half the effects would be felt.

Product Price and Real Wage Changes

In this calculation I have applied a conventional net-factor-content approach. Deardorff and Staiger have shown that with fairly strong assumptions about consumption patterns and production functions (namely, that product expenditures and factor shares remain constant shares of income), the change in relative wages will be proportional to the changes in total relative factor supplies represented by changes in the net factor content of trade.[4] Thus this approach provides a useful benchmark for estimating the effects.

The Stolper-Samuelson theorem of trade tells one that in this scenario the real wage of skilled workers will rise and the real wage of unskilled workers will fall. One knows, therefore, that if the relative wage of unskilled workers falls by about 7 percent, the real wage will fall by less than 7 percent. To obtain explicit relative price and real wage effects associated with this scenario, Carolyn Evans and I have approximated the scenario discussed above, using a general equilibrium, two-factor, three-sector model.[5] The model has a nontraded goods sector that accounts for 82.5 percent of consumption, and high-skill and basic manufacturing industries that account for 10.0 and 7.5 percent, respectively. It

4. Deardorff and Staiger (1988). See also Krugman (1995a) for a particularly elegant derivation.
5. Lawrence and Evans (1996).

has Cobb-Douglas production and consumption functions and is para-
meterized using the data in table 6-1.[6] The nontraded and high-skill
sectors each use similar ratios of high-school and college workers, while
the basic sector is more high-school intensive. Trade is always balanced.

In the simulation the economy starts from a position of self-sufficiency
in which production corresponds to the U.S. production in 1990. The
economy is then provided the opportunity to trade at given alternative
world prices. As the world price of the basic-industry product falls, the
economy responds by moving along the frontier of its production possibilities, reducing its basic-industry production, and expanding its exports
of high-skill products. In the simulation that is relevant here, the United
States has moved to the point where it has just eliminated production in
the basic sector and has specialized in high-skill manufacturing production. In this simulation it turns out that the output of the high-skill sector
expands by 83.2 percent and nontraded goods output by 4.7 percent.

As Dae Il Kim and Peter Mieszkowski have emphasized, an aggregate
production possibilities curve such as the one here, in which the sectors
have fairly similar Cobb-Douglas production functions, is remarkably
flat.[7] To bring about this fairly large shift in resources, an increase in the
relative price of high-skill (and nontraded goods) of only about 2 percent
is required. This is itself an interesting result, since it helps explain why
studies examining relative price changes have not found evidence of large
changes in the past.

However, as Kim and Mieszkowski also stress, when sectors use relatively similar input ratios, small changes in relative prices will have large
magnification effects on relative factor prices. The 2 percent shift in
relative prices is associated with a decline in the ratio of skilled to unskilled wages of 7.5 percent. This is basically the same as the estimate of
7.5 percent shown by the net-factor-content exercise above. This result
demonstrates how the net-factor-content approach gives the same answer
as a general equilibrium simulation based on conventional trade theory.[8]
Absolute wages are also of interest. In this simulation the real wages of
skilled workers rise by 3.3 percent, while the real wages of unskilled
workers fall by 4.4 percent. Since skilled workers earn more than unskilled workers, the gains to skilled workers exceed the losses of unskilled

6. The shares in output of high-school workers' earnings in the basic, high-tech, and
nontraded industries are 0.65, 0.40, and 0.40, respectively.

7. Kim and Mieszkowski (1995).

8. For an elegant proof see Krugman (1995b).

workers—the economy as a whole gains from trade—but by a very small amount.

As one would expect from the Stolper-Samuelson theorem, therefore, unskilled workers are hurt by trade. The upper-bound estimate in this scenario is a fall in real wages of 4.4 percent. Since this impact would be felt over fifteen years, if average real wages in the United States were to rise by 1 percent a year because of higher domestic productivity, workers could absorb the change due to trade and still experience a real earnings growth of 0.84 percent annually. I should emphasize, however, that the results here are sensitive to the assumptions made about the parameters that characterize consumption and production relationships. In particular, with less elastic production and demand functions, the impact of relative prices and wages would be larger.[9] Nonetheless, as the discussion in chapter 2 dealing with Adrian Wood's methodology makes clear, assumptions of unitary elasticities for demand and unitary substitution elasticities can be readily defended.

Qualifications

While useful as a first effort, several questions can legitimately be raised about this scenario:

ELASTICITY PARAMETERS. Unitary elasticities are appealing from a computational viewpoint, but are they realistic? Lawrence Katz and Kevin Murphy provide an estimate of 1.41, while others—for example, Adrian Wood and Jeffrey Sachs and Howard Shatz—favor much lower estimates of about -0.5.[10] Note, however, that there are two senses in which this elasticity of substitution between factors of production is used. Many econometric estimates of the elasticity of substitution probably capture not only the pure factor substitution effect in producing a given product but also the effects induced by different factor prices on product mix and quality. (See Wood for a discussion.) For my purposes, however, the broader effect is relevant, leading me to accept estimates of the elasticity in the range of unity.

9. See Rowthorn (1994) for a variety of simulations in a general equilibrium framework.

10. Katz and Murphy (1992); Wood (1994); Sachs and Shatz (forthcoming). Wood summarizes the literature as providing estimates of between 1 and 2 but favors using 0.5 on the grounds that these are contaminated by the induced effects of shifts in product mix. However, in the case of a forward-looking simulation, this is not necessarily inappropriate.

Carolyn Evans and I have simulated the impact with lower elasticities of substitution in production.[11] With an elasticity of 0.5 there are relative prices of 4.1 percent and relative wages of 14.9 percent, split between a decline in real wages of high-school workers by 9.1 percent and an increase in real college wages by 6.9 percent.

GROWTH. By using data from 1990, I have ignored the fact that over a fifteen-year period there will be productivity improvements and the economy is likely to grow. Indeed, over a fifteen-year period, with output per worker in manufacturing increasing at the 2.5 percent annual rate it averaged between 1979 and 1994, for example, the employment impact of these shifts would be reduced by 44 percent. (Alternatively, we could think of these as scenarios in which developing-country trade volumes could be larger by 44 percent to have the estimated effects.) Taking productivity growth into account, therefore, suggests that an 11.3 percent annual growth rate over fifteen years in imports from developing countries would reduce the relative demand for high-school workers by 0. 56 × 7.5, or 4.1 percent, in the case of a unitary elasticity of substitution and by 9.2 percent with an elasticity of substitution equal to 0.5. This would imply declines in real high-school wages of between 2.5 and 6.2 percent. This is therefore a more realistic estimate of the displacement effects of the volume effects in the scenario.

Second, the U.S. labor force is likely to grow over this period at an annual rate of about 1 percent. This implies that the employment shifts represented by these trade flows will constitute relatively smaller shares of the labor force. Assuming a proportional increase in the ratio of high-school to college workers, that would reduce the estimates of relative wage changes implied by these trade volumes of an additional 15 percent, that is, to 0.85 × 4.1, or 3.5 percent, with unitary elasticities and 7.82 percent with an elasticity of substitution of 0.5, yielding real wage declines of between 2.1 and 5.3 percent, accounting for both growth and productivity changes.

INDUCED DEMAND AND SUPPLY. Third, I have taken the relative supplies and demands for these factors as given. But there are likely to be responses in both demand and supply that will reduce this effect. On the demand side, technological innovation could occur that saves on the use

11. Lawrence and Evans (1996).

of college workers and makes more intensive use of high-school workers. On the supply side, the lower relative wage of high-school workers implies an increase in the return to education. If the lower wage induces workers and new labor-force entrants to invest more in education, that will reduce the relative supply of high-school workers and bolster their relative wages. The net result would therefore be a shift that is smaller than 4.1 percent over fifteen years.

RENTS. The simulations have assumed that the average wages earned by high-school and college workers are the same throughout the economy. But, in fact, there are differences. Lawrence Katz and Lawrence Summers have estimated the wage premiums for two-digit manufacturing industries for managers and laborers.[12] Ascribing their estimates of rents for managers to college workers and for laborers to high-school workers suggests that, on average, the rents of managers and workers in basic industries are 6 and 2 percent, respectively, while for college and high-school workers in high-skill industries on average they are 15 and 13 percent, respectively. Thus, given these rents, the shift in employment from the basic to the high-skill sector would increase average rents for both types of workers. That would be the source of additional gains from trade.[13] On average, for employment shifts laid out in the net-factor-content scenario described above, average economywide rents earned by high-school and college workers would rise by 0.7 and 0.8 percent, respectively. Taking these increases into account therefore leaves the impact of trade on relative wages unchanged, but implies a decline of 3.6 percent (4.4 − 0.8) in real wages of unskilled workers in the face of a fivefold increase in import volumes (assuming a unity substitution elasticity).

Aggregation Level

The highly aggregative nature of the scenario may be questioned. But the scenario is not to be taken literally; it is meant to be illustrative rather than precise. Undoubtedly many sectors and firms in the basic industries are highly skill intensive, and some in the high-skill sector may be vulnerable to international competition. But as long as the orders of magnitude are not biased, that should not matter.

12. Katz and Summers (1989).
13. Indeed, Katz and Summers find that U.S. export industries provide higher wage premiums than those competing with imports.

In addition, the kinds of products that are initially eliminated through international competition may be more high-school intensive on average than the typical basic industry. Similarly, exports might be disproportionately concentrated in sectors with relatively lower high-school employment ratios. In contrast to the impact of taking productivity into account, this might affect the timing of the required adjustments, bringing them forward in time rather than pushing them off (as occurs in the scenario with growing effects over time). However, once the more labor-intensive sectors are eliminated, the net employment effects become smaller, because the sectors become increasingly similar in relative employment intensities.

I have taken account only of value-added in manufacturing. Of course, import-competing products and exports contain value-added from other sectors. One assumption that would allow this calculation to be retained is that the nonmanufacturing components of value-added have employment ratios similar to those for manufacturing. The $552 billion dollars could then be taken as a change inside and outside manufacturing, and thus an even larger volume of trade and larger effects might be expected before all basic industries were eliminated. However, it is likely that the service inputs into basic and high-skill industries are more alike than the manufacturing inputs.

Adjustment Costs

The model has ignored the costs of adjustment. For individual workers these could be significant, but even assuming that for each displaced worker they were the equivalent of one year's annual income, the displacement costs of an additional 8 percent of the labor force over a period of fifteen years are a relatively small size of the average wage bill. For high-school workers, who account for three-quarters of those displaced, such a loss would amount to less than half a percent of the average total wage bill each year.

Services Trade

Finally, there is the issue of nonmanufactured-goods trade. In several areas improvements in communications have increased the scope of what may be traded. In particular, as an example in the low-skill area, data-processing activities once performed domestically in OECD countries are increasingly undertaken abroad. Even high-skill firms are finding it feasible to use software and other talented engineers in developing countries. Nonetheless, if the experience in goods trade is indicative, it remains likely that services trade between OECD and developing countries will occur mainly along skill lines, with the OECD exporting skill-intensive services and importing unskilled-intensive services.

The literature on the potential for providing long-distance services has been surveyed by the World Bank.[14] They report studies showing that an estimated 12 to 16 percent of those employed in services in the Group of Seven (G-7) countries engage in services that could, technically, be provided at long distance. However, there are many activities that for strategic reasons, such as preserving proprietary information, companies are reluctant to outsource, particularly internationally. The Bank therefore estimates that between 1 and 5 percent of the total employment in services in the G-7 economies is contestable internationally and that the potential market for such exports in the United States in 1990 dollars is roughly between $14 billion and $43 billion, and in all the G-7 countries between $40 billion and $120 billion. Even though the high estimate of $43 billion represents about 30 percent of the value of U.S. manufactured imports in 1990, if the internationally contestable share remained a similar proportion of employment over the next fifteen years, it would be too small to have a major effect on the calculations in this scenario. Apparently, therefore, most employment outside manufacturing will remain nontraded.

Conclusion

In summary, this exercise suggests that over a fifteen-year period rapid increases in U.S. trade with developing countries could depress the relative and absolute wages of unskilled U.S. workers. In its most stark form, once productivity growth is taken into account, the effects are on the order of about a 2.5 percent decline in real wages over the period and an effect that is even smaller once the impact of wage premiums in the export sector is accounted for. In an economy in which average real wage growth was fairly strong, this type of change, of about a sixth of a percent a year, would not be a major issue, particularly if there were positive effects on the less-skilled because of other changes in the labor

14. World Bank (1995, chapter 3).

market. But if that change is combined with continued strength in skill-biased technological and organizational change, dealing with unskilled workers will present an important challenge for policy.

It should be emphasized, however, that such an outcome is an upper-bound impact. It ignores the fact that trade may bring benefits by increasing scale economies, enhancing competition, transferring technology, and increasing product diversity, all of which could *raise* the wages of both high-school and college graduates. It also ignores the fact that poorer workers are more likely to consume the price-sensitive basic goods whose prices will fall as a result of trade. Moreover, once the economy eliminates domestic production of the basic industries in which the developing countries specialize, additional increases in world supplies of these products would *increase the real wages of all American workers* by providing them with cheaper imports.[15] Additional trade with developing countries would then not necessarily affect wage inequality in the United States—although given the relatively small shares of imported goods in consumption, this effect should not be exaggerated. One implied message, therefore, is that although there may be some effect on inequality, in the long run trade with developing countries should provide benefits to all who live in the OECD.

Finally, this simulation about the future also contains an implicit, but very important, lesson about the past. If the impact of very large shifts in trade in the future is likely to be relatively small, it suggests that the much smaller growth in trade with developing countries over the past fifteen years is unlikely to have had the serious impact on labor markets in the OECD that many claim it has.

---

15. If the developing countries shift into high-skill products, on the other hand, the U.S. terms of trade could decline.

CHAPTER SEVEN

Policy Implications and Conclusion

IN THIS STUDY I have found that unskilled workers have borne the brunt of the poor labor-market performance in OECD countries since the mid-1970s. But trade with developing countries has played a relatively small role in accounting for this performance. Changes in manufacturing production techniques and, for the United States, the decline in productivity growth in the services sector, appear to be far more important. I have also suggested that in the future trade could have a negative effect on the welfare of less-skilled workers, but that its effects are likely to be relatively small, primarily because the number of adversely affected workers is small compared with the number of unskilled workers whose jobs are in sectors that are sheltered from developing-country trade.

Here I discuss some policy implications of these findings. I begin the chapter with a discussion of international labor standards. I then discuss briefly other policies—trade protection, education and training, and income redistribution—before providing some general conclusions.

Labor Standards

In most OECD countries the government has an extensive role in the labor market. It commonly regulates work hours and the cost of overtime; mandates public holidays and sick leave; sets minimum wages; restricts child and forced labor; ensures nondiscrimination; provides unemployment, disability, and retirement income insurance and, in many countries, health insurance; and sets conditions for hiring and firing, unionization, and collective bargaining.

By and large, nations have taken these actions independently, although a voluntary set of international standards has been agreed to at International Labor Organization (ILO) conventions. The General Agreement on Tariffs and Trade (GATT) contains only a fairly narrow prohibition on trade in goods made with forced labor.[1] In addition, the United States has used "core" labor standards, and the European Union plans in 1998 to use labor standards, as a criterion for granting trade preferences under their generalized system of preferences for developing countries (GSP).[2]

Efforts to bring these issues to the international policy arena have been made in both the United States and the European Union. As early as 1953 the United States proposed adding a labor-standards article to GATT, and it pushed unsuccessfully for the inclusion of labor standards in the Tokyo and Uruguay Rounds. The United States has also tried to induce foreign compliance with worker rights in other aspects of its trade policy. Since the mid-1980s the U.S. Congress has passed a series of laws that directly link preferential trade and investment benefits to respect for basic worker rights.[3] In section 301 and super 301 of the Omnibus Trade Act of 1988, the "systematic denial of internationally recognized worker rights" by foreign governments is defined as an "unreasonable trade practice" and made liable for U.S. countermeasures where "such denials cause a burden or restrictions on U.S. commerce." Labor standards were also an important issue in the negotiations on the North American Free

1. The original charter of the International Trade Organization in 1948 contained a section on labor rights, although it was never ratified by the U.S. Congress for other reasons.

2. Core labor standards are defined as the right of association; the right to organize and bargain collectively; a prohibition against forced labor; appropriate restrictions on child labor; and nondiscrimination, for example on grounds of age, sex, and race. Jackson, Davey, and Sykes (1995, p. 999).

3. Eligibility under the Caribbean Basin Economic Recovery Act of 1983, the GSP in 1984, the Overseas Private Investment Corporation in 1985, and 1987 U.S. participation in the Multilateral Investment Guarantee Agency have all been conditioned on a minimum set of internationally recognized standards on worker rights that include the rights to associate and bargain collectively, the banning of forced or compulsory or child labor, the provision of reasonable conditions for worker health and safety, and the existence of a national mechanism for determining a generally applicable minimum wage. These standards are modeled on ILO conventions.

Trade Agreement. Although NAFTA itself does not include provisions on labor rights, one of the side agreements is aimed at strengthening enforcement of national labor standards. In particular, it has established a trinational enforcement regime for alleged violations of national minimum wage, child labor, and occupational health and safety regulations, and an oversight and evaluation mechanism (without enforcement powers) for other labor issues.[4] More recently, because of the 1994 change in the composition of the U.S. Congress, labor standards have become a matter of contention, with the Democratic administration seeking to include labor standards in its fast-track authority to negotiate additional regional free trade agreements and the more conservative Republican Congress resisting such action.

The U.S. focus in international agreements has been on achieving "minimum, internationally recognized standards." By contrast, measures within the European Community—and now the European Union—have been more extensive. In 1956, according to B. Steil, French officials argued that social legislation in Europe should be harmonized in conjunction with the reduction of tariff protection to "make apparent to the workers the link that must exist between the common market's establishment and higher standards of living."[5] More recently, European countries that fail to provide their workers with "adequate social protection" are widely viewed as guilty of "social dumping". On December 9, 1989, all EC members except Britain agreed to the Social Charter, which covers an extensive set of worker's rights.[6] The European Commission has also been active in implementing this charter.[7]

4. Conspicuous by their absence, and an important reason for the opposition of organized U.S. labor to NAFTA, were rights of association, organizing, and bargaining.

5. Steil (1994, p. 15).

6. These include rights to freedom of movement; employment and remuneration; the improvement of living and working conditions—the right to social protection; the right to freedom of association and collective bargaining; the right to vocational training; the right of men and women to equal treatment; the right to information, consultation, and participation; the right to health and safety in the workplace; the protection of children and adolescents in employment; the protection of elderly persons; and the protection of persons with disabilities.

7. The Single European Act allows social-policy measures relating to the health and safety of workers to be adopted by a qualified majority, while requiring unanimity in other areas of social policy. The Commission has accordingly defined a working-time directive (which requires a maximum forty-eight-hour work week and four-week annual paid vacation) as a "health and safety" measure. Of course, in Europe a key quid pro quo to members with lower wage levels is access to the cohesion fund.

At a multilateral level there are increasing calls for moving beyond the voluntary standards of the ILO and the GATT's prohibition on forced labor.[8] The United States tried to ensure that discussions on labor standards would take place in the new World Trade Organization. French leaders have been vocal in calling for European action against other nations with lower standards of social protection. Former prime minister Edouard Balladur of France, for example, demanded that Europe be protected from "foreign traders with different values."

If the central finding of this study, that trade with developing countries has not had a major impact on OECD labor markets, is accepted, it implies a fortiori that differences between the OECD and developing countries in either wage levels or labor standards have not played a major role. Therefore, whatever the merits of an international agreement on such labor standards, it is unlikely to be an important instrument for reducing either wage inequality or unemployment within the OECD. If the case for labor standards is to be made, it should be made on other grounds. What might these grounds be? I first consider arguments that focus on efficiency and the principles of market failure. Then I turn to arguments based on other considerations.

It is useful to distinguish conceptually three types of effects that labor policies might have: those that are purely local; those that operate on international markets through market spillovers; and those that operate on international markets through direct spillovers.[9]

Local Effects

Where nations effectively control their borders and prevent immigration, most labor standards either will be only felt locally or will operate through market channels to affect international trade and investment flows. In fact, despite the widespread perception that such policies have repercussions on trade and investment flows, in many cases government intervention in the labor market will have purely local impacts.

First, policies such as sick leave, maternity leave, and family leave are usually financed by payroll taxes. It is often assumed that such taxes on labor raise employment costs, thereby affecting resource allocation. But unless all elements of the compensation package, including wages, are

8. See Collingsworth, Goold, and Harvey (1994).

9. I owe this classification scheme to Richard Cooper's analysis of global environmental policies. See Cooper (1993).

subject to minimum standards, when such standards are imposed, employers can adjust other elements of the package to keep their total costs from rising substantially. Indeed, the evidence suggests that in general the supply of labor is fairly inelastic and that over the long run most payroll taxes are borne by labor.[10] This implies that such taxes result in lower wages rather than higher compensation costs.[11] To the extent that payroll taxes are shifted back to workers in the form of lower wages, they would not affect trade or investment flows.

Second, some labor measures reflect decisions that might have been taken in the marketplace anyway, and are thus not binding constraints. This could be true of rules about work hours, vacation, and minimum wages. Also, in many countries compliance with binding measures is low and enforcement weak. Under some circumstances evasion takes the form of employment in the informal sector.[12] These considerations are both important, reminding us that the basic presumption that differences in labor standards will affect trade and investment flows is not necessarily valid.

Market Forces

In practice, however, other labor market policies will not be perfectly neutral. In fact, their impact can be subtle. Ronald Ehrenberg gives the example of payroll taxes with ceilings, which can shift demand toward more highly paid workers.[13] Similarly, some employment standards are not fully shiftable; for example, a binding minimum wage or child labor laws. If the value employees place on health and safety benefits is less than the employers' costs of complying with them, only part of the costs will be shifted back in the form of lower wages.

Under these circumstances, standards will affect costs, and costs will in turn affect trade and investment flows.[14] Countries with labor stan-

10. OECD (1993).

11. Some labor standards may actually increase the supply of labor and enhance productivity. Thus a safer workplace may raise work-force participation, and the increased unionization and worker participation in decisionmaking could increase productivity.

12. Ehrenberg (1994) notes that the substantial differences in benefit levels prevailing across the United States show that even within an integrated market there is considerable scope for exercizing local preferences. Maximum weekly unemployment insurance varies from $154 in Nebraska to $468 in Massachusetts.

13. Ehrenberg (1994).

14. For some empirical estimates of the impact of labor standards, see Rodrik (forthcoming).

dards that raise costs could change the goods in which they are internationally competitive. Moreover, these pressures will occur largely in sectors in which foreigners can offer similar products at lower costs.

In general, therefore, groups seeking to raise labor standards will find that their case becomes more difficult the higher the costs they impose on society. It should therefore come as no surprise that such groups might oppose trade and investment liberalization, particularly with trading partners that have very different preferences. But countries adopt many social regulations and policies even though they might affect costs. And if one country believes in the utility of such standards, it should surely be free to implement them and to bear the costs. Unless they provide offsetting productivity benefits, the costs of higher standards must be borne by someone. This would require an offsetting decline in incomes, which could occur either directly, through lowering wages or profits, or indirectly, through a depreciation in the exchange rate.

If one accepts the principle of national sovereignty, as long as nations are small and part of an open world economy, allowing them to determine these standards independently will lead to an optimal allocation of resources. As Lawrence, Albert Bressand, and Takatoshi Ito elaborate, the traditional theory of international trade demonstrates that when costs differ, countries gain from free trade by specializing along the lines of comparative advantage.[15] When David Ricardo invoked the principle of comparative advantage, he referred to productive differences that were due to climate (or technology).[16] But in stating his theory, Ricardo could as easily have ascribed the productive differences between nations to the social climate as to the physical climate, and his conclusions would have been unchanged: *Taking climatic conditions as given, free trade will maximise global welfare.*

The choices of sovereign nation states are reflected in part in their rules and regulations. These regulatory decisions certainly influence relative costs and thus patterns of comparative advantage. Given diversity of national conditions and regulatory preferences, however, it is optimal for nations to have *different* regulations and norms. In the light of this paradigm, therefore, those seeking more level playing fields based on

15. Lawrence, Bressand, and Ito (1996).
16. These explanations for trade have been so widely invoked that people sometimes treat as a "refutation" of the principle of comparative advantage the discovery that institutions and policies can also affect comparative advantage, so that comparative advantage can actually be "created" by governments.

constraining domestic economic policies in other countries fail to understand that the benefits of international trade come from allowing nations to be different, rather than requiring them to be similar.

As with all paradigms, however, this view of the world rests on some basic assumptions. If these assumptions are violated, unconstrained free trade may not be globally optimal. In particular, two assumptions are crucial. The first is that the world consists of perfectly functioning, competitive markets—that is, that there are no international market failures. The second is the normative proposition that no constraints should be imposed on sovereign national choices (an assumption analogous to consumer sovereignty).

Spillovers

Markets may fail, however, where there are externalities. Labor-market regulations and programs in one country may directly affect conditions in a second country through induced labor flows. Immigration creates problems, for example, when workers from one country can receive benefits but not pay the costs of such benefits in a second country. Under these circumstances, since the spillovers are not simply pecuniary, the case for an increased harmonization (or mutual recognition) of policies is considerably stronger. It is thus not surprising that, as it perfects its internal labor market, the European Union has moved to implement more extensive sets of common standards.

Monopolistic Power

The assumption of competitive global markets is important because it rules out the use of strategic labor-standard policies; namely, policies designed to achieve a given impact not only on the labor market but also on the nation's terms of trade. As Drusilla Brown, Alan Deardorff, and Robert Stern demonstrate, with market power a labor standard could operate like an optimal tariff and shift the terms of trade.[17] For example, South Africa could raise the price and reduce the supply of gold in the world by raising safety standards in its gold mines.[18] In the presence of this potential, international controls on standard setting might be required.

17. Brown, Deardorff, and Stern (1993).
18. Exporting countries have incentives to set standards too high globally because they

In the real world, however, most labor-standard policy decisions are not motivated by terms-of-trade considerations, and accusations of the use of labor standards for such purposes are rare. Indeed, exporters of labor-intensive products are likely to have lower standards and importers higher standards because concerns about employment tend to dominate those of maximizing aggregate national income.

Political Failure

Instead, the more compelling challenges to complete national sovereignty are based on (a) the notion that there exist basic universal human rights and (b) the "psychological externalities" that occur when citizens of one country find practices in other countries morally reprehensible.

In particularly egregious cases, some nations have challenged the principle that others should enjoy untrammeled sovereignty when in comes to human rights. Indeed, these challenges have at times involved not only trade sanctions, such as sanctions against the apartheid regime in South Africa, but also military intervention. Nonetheless, where the line should be drawn remains highly controversial. It is apparent from the number of countries that have voluntarily signed the labor-standards conventions of the ILO that there is a widespread international consensus on several basic standards. It is a leap, however, from countries agreeing themselves to adhere to principles to allowing others to use trade as an enforcement mechanism to ensure that they do. Generally, therefore, aside from egregious cases, the international community has been wary of using for punitive measures to enforce human rights.

It may be better in some cases to use rewards rather than sanctions. Indeed, the policies in poor countries that offend the sensibilities of those in rich nations result from different income levels (that is, income effects) rather than different preferences or values. Thus those in extreme poverty may permit activities that under other circumstances they themselves would regard as abhorrent, such as child labor or a lack of pollution controls. The long-run solution to these problems is clearly to raise incomes. Refusing to trade with such nations could retard rather than improve their abilities to provide worker rights. In the short run, however, some of these conflicts can be dealt with through explicit compensation schemes and subsidies. For

---

receive this secondary terms-of-trade benefit. Importing countries would do the opposite. This counterintuitive result implies that labor-intensive exporters should set standards too high. See Brown, Deardorff, and Stern (1993).

example, the European Union has a set of social funds that allow poorer countries to meet the labor and social standards applied by more affluent members. Similarly, "debt for nature" swaps allow richer nations to support environmental activities in poorer countries.

In other cases countries may trade off their adherence to particular practices by obtaining concessions in other areas; for example, in the Uruguay Round some developing countries agreed to the introduction of intellectual property rules in return for increased market access in textiles and agriculture. NAFTA provides another example in which Mexico signed a (side) agreement on labor standards in return for preferential market access. As noted, the United States has conditioned access to preferential arrangements, such as GSP, on adherence to basic labor standards.

Where sufficient compensation is not forthcoming, however, there is a danger in trying to impose such standards under conditions in which they may damage economic growth. Moreover, cases will remain in which divergent practices reflect divergent beliefs about the desirability of such standards, so that compensation will not be possible; for instance, the conflicts between the United States and the Soviet Union over Jewish emigration and those between the United States and China over human rights. Under these circumstances free trade may be difficult to obtain. And indeed, by revealed preference, both nations may be better off without such trade.

Nevertheless, even when governments chose neither to sanction nor reward, private citizens in developed countries could be given the ability to exercise their preferences through the market. An alternative to sanctions might be an insistence on labeling (such as "made with union workers" or "made using ecologically sound standards") that would allow private citizens to exercise their preferences. Those willing to pay more to exert their moral sensitivities should be allowed to do so.

On the other hand, when nations agree on core standards, particularly in a multilateral setting where diverse interests are represented, international agreements can help make such standards more credible domestically and reduce the opportunity and adjustment costs of imposing them alone. Moreover, the presence of a reasonable set of mutually agreed minimum standards could help reduce the ability for political interests to exploit these concerns for protectionist purposes.

In sum, in general a strong case exists for allowing individual nations a wide scope for differentiation in applying labor standards, particularly when the costs and benefits of such standards are fully borne by the nation itself. Even when these standards do affect others through market forces, in principle, given diverse social preferences, the existence of diverse standards will raise global welfare. There is, however, a case for international standards when (a) there is a strong danger that nations would act strategically in their absence; (b) nations can agree on what those standards should be; or (c) nations share a common labor market. When the failure to maintain certain standards impinges on notions of fundamental human rights, they are more difficult to deal with. One solution is to induce poor nations to comply by offering them compensation. A second is to use labeling and other forms of moral suasion. The denial of trading opportunities should probably come only as a last resort and only in the most egregious cases. Nonetheless, whatever is agreed on internationally, the impact on labor-market performance should not be exaggerated.

Trade Policy

In principle, even if technological changes and changes in management practices, rather than trade, are the source of growing inequality, trade protection could be used to shift the distribution of income if that was deemed a desirable social goal. As I discussed earlier, the Stolper-Samuelson theorem predicts that a tariff that raises the price of unskilled-labor-intensive goods, for example, would increase the relative wages of unskilled workers. But as every textbook on international economics demonstrates, trade protection is an inefficient way to achieve such redistribution because, besides redistributing income, it distorts the decisions of both consumers and producers.[19] It will usually be far more efficient to redistribute income directly through taxes and transfers than to do so indirectly by using trade protection. The use of transfers not only would be more efficient for OECD countries but would also avoid the highly damaging impact that a shift toward OECD protection would have on developing countries.

Imposing trade protection on developing countries would mean playing the experience over the past fifteen years in reverse. Since trade has apparently not had a great impact on income distribution in the past, an increase in protection sufficient to reverse the growth in imports from

19. Bhagwati (1971).

developing countries over the past fifteen years would not have a great impact on relative wages. Moreover, any given level of protection would provide only one-time relief if it was used to redress the inequality brought about by other causes. Once protection had been raised, these other causes, such as technological and organizational changes and the relatively rapid increase in productivity growth in manufacturing, would continue.

An alternative approach to dealing with international competition from developing countries is to try to facilitate, rather than resist, the adjustment.[20] As noted in chapter 6, if the production of goods that compete directly with those produced by developing countries is eliminated, only the positive benefits from such trade will remain. Indeed, whereas protection brings a one-time benefit that will subsequently be offset by a sequence of costs, this form of trade adjustment brings a one-time cost that is subsequently offset by a sequence of benefits if import prices continue to fall. This adjustment would be promoted by lowering rather than raising trade barriers. That approach is being followed at both the regional (for example, NAFTA) and global levels (for example, the Uruguay Round agreement). Such a policy could be complemented with improved facilities in the labor market to assist workers in finding new jobs, and with policies favorable both to the development and diffusion of technology and to firms' attempts to make the transition to more flexible forms of organization.[21]

Education and Training

Another policy strategy involves measures to increase education and training. To some extent, market forces will do this automatically. When the relative wages of uneducated workers fall, the returns to education implicitly rise. To take an extreme example. If workers with low levels of education in OECD countries saw their wages fall to levels equal to those of workers in developing countries, they would have tremendous incentives to invest in education. In part, therefore, the automatic supply responses in the labor market will help unwind some of the inequality seen in the United States and the United Kingdom by encouraging workers to investment in their skills and education. Increasing the relative

20. For a more detailed discussion, see Lawrence and Litan (1986).
21. See Oman (1996) for further discussion of the transition problem.

supply of educated workers should, in turn, drive up the relative wages of unskilled workers. In continental Europe and Japan, however, wages have not become dispersed along skill lines. Thus for employed workers there are less incentives to invest in skills acquisition. To the degree that skilled workers suffer more unemployment, however, there will be an increased return to education—although if unemployment compensation is generous, this effect may be mitigated or offset. But there are compelling reasons to believe that the market for human capital does not work perfectly. In particular, without government assistance many individuals may lack the means to finance their education. Unlike firms, for example, individuals cannot finance their acquisition of knowledge by issuing equity. In addition, education may provide social benefits that are not fully captured by those who are educated. These positive externalities from education suggest that it should be subsidized and promoted in any case.

Nonetheless, particularly for older workers who may be difficult to train, education will not be a panacea. Yet if education is provided only to younger, new labor-market entrants, it would take a long time before the benefits of improved education were felt throughout the economy. Moreover, to be effective in closing the earnings gap between skilled and unskilled workers, training should be directed disproportionately toward lower-skilled workers. In fact, as Lisa Lynch has shown, these workers are the least likely to receive post-school training in the United States, and the training such workers do receive from their employees is often of a firm-specific character.[22] Instead, firms seem to spend a disproportionate share of their training dollars improving the skills of workers who are most easily educated, namely those who have already acquired higher education. This suggests that if governments are interested in improving equality, they should concentrate on the skills acquisition of the less skilled.

Income Redistribution

Another avenue for policy is income redistribution. One approach is to focus narrowly on trade. In the United States doing so is still feasible by using the trade adjustment assistance program. Workers laid off because of trade are treated differently from others. However, trade adjustment assistance can be given only to those actually displaced by trade

22. Lynch (1995).

and will not help in dealing with losses to the wages of employed workers. For these workers, devices such as the earned-income tax credit or progressive taxation in general may have a role to play.

As noted, in Europe unskilled workers appear to have done poorly by losing their jobs and experiencing higher unemployment than in the United States. Nevertheless, such workers may experience less relative poverty, because wage structures tend to be more rigid and income supports to the unemployed are relatively more generous than in the United States. In the United States the unskilled seem to do better in terms of employment opportunities but only at relatively lower wages. In continental Europe's more rigid system, workers apparently do better in terms of income but worse in terms of employment opportunities. An ideal policy would combine the flexibility of the labor market in the United States with the levels of income support provided in Europe.

One way to implement such a policy is to build on the earned income tax credit which has been in operation in the United States for some time. This approach is a form of negative income tax, tied to income earned from labor. It allows the labor market to set wages at rates that reflect supply and demand, but it provides a supplement to full-time workers whose earnings fall below certain levels. The credit begins to phase out slowly, to avoid raising the implicit marginal tax rate, once earnings rise above a certain level. A credit provided in this form heightens the incentive to work and achieves redistribution that is related to wage earnings without major distortions in the labor market. Revenues allocated to this measure could be increased in the United States, and if introduced in Europe, it might allow for the relaxation of legal provisions that currently limit wage flexibility.

Another approach, which has been followed in Europe, is to increase socially provided public goods such as health care, child care, and education. These raise the well-being of workers and in principle could be financed by progressive income taxes. But given the need for fiscal restraint in most OECD countries, this approach is less practical in today's circumstances.

Conclusions

In general, the impact of globalization on OECD labor markets has been far less significant or damaging than many have argued. Trade has played no role in the sluggish growth in average U.S. wages over the past two decades, a development that reflects the slowdown in U.S. productivity growth outside manufacturing. Trade appears to have played some role in employment shifts, however, particularly in the declining employment opportunities in labor-intensive sectors such as apparel. Nonetheless, as estimated by conventional net-factor-content methods, over the 1980s these effects remained too small to account for more than about 10 to 15 percent (that is, 1.5 percentage points) of the differential that emerged between high-school and college workers in the United States, and very little of the unemployment that emerged in the United Kingdom and Germany. Moreover, trade contributed positively to employment in Japan.

Adrian Wood has offered a critique of conventional net-factor-content methods and provided alternative estimates that give trade with the South a much larger role. But his work rests on an assumption that is not credible—namely, that the North and South have similar technological capabilities; his counterfactual simulations use unrealistically low-elasticity parameters; and his assertions about the magnitudes of induced productivity growth are not supported by evidence. Indeed, with more realistic assumptions about price elasticities, Wood's model would give results that are similar to those obtained by conventional estimates. Moreover, the literature suggests that trade has had an impact on productivity growth, but only in concentrated industries—which are not those in which developing countries typically specialize.

The minor role played by trade is also suggested by the behavior of the prices of traded goods in the 1980s. The negative relationship that might have been expected between import prices and the use of unskilled labor is not present in either trade or domestic price data for the United States, Germany, and Japan. It is not present for measures of skill either by occupation (that is, production-nonproduction workers) or by education.

Nor is there much evidence to support the view that trade operates on economywide relative wages by altering relative industry wage premiums. General specifications do find a negative relationship between trade and industry wages in the United States, but the effects are relatively small. There is also evidence of some responsiveness in union and other premiums in concentrated industries, although these have often been positive rather than negative. In the United States specifically, workers with high-school degrees in high-rent industries (or union members) have experienced only minor declines in relative earnings. Nor has trade resulted in the erosion of sufficiently large numbers of high-rent jobs to have depressed the average (economywide) relative earnings of high-school graduates by reducing their employment in high-rent manufacturing sectors.

The evidence drawn from data on U.S. multinationals shows that commonly shared technological and organizational changes have had a greater impact on the economy than trade and international outsourcing. Employment fell in both U.S. parents and their affiliates in developed countries, and grew only modestly in developing countries. In foreign affiliates in both developed and developing countries, the relative compensation of nonproduction workers increased and the ratio of production to nonproduction workers fell, a result consistent with the argument of a pervasive shift in manufacturing production techniques and organizational structures that has increased the use and rewards of educated workers. Although U.S. parent sourcing from overseas affiliates grew rapidly, the increase accounted for only a small share of total sales.

International trade enhances potential national welfare. It frees up resources to be put to alternative uses in which they are more productive. But for these benefits to be realized, it is necessary that those resources do not remain unemployed. In several labor markets, particularly in Europe, the loss of a job is viewed with anxiety. The result is that increased trade, or technological progress, is seen as a threat rather than an opportunity. In this book, however, I have shown there is considerable empirical evidence that the sources of poor labor-market performance are essentially domestic. They reflect ongoing technological and organizational shocks that would be present even if the economy were closed. The role of developing-country imports and the sourcing activities of U.S. multinationals both remain too small to account for a significant share of the relative wage changes that have occurred in the United States. This evidence implies that international differences either in wage rates or in labor standards are not the major factors in OECD labor-market behavior that many believe them to be.

These findings suggest that the main challenges to policy are to educate the public on the nature of the changes; to emphasize the need for worker training and education to take advantage of the opportunities new technologies and new organizational structures afford; and to develop measures such as earned-income tax credits that redress earnings inequality while preserving and increasing wage flexibility.

Finally, when nations share a common consensus on labor standards, as most do with respect to core standards, there is probably merit in reinforcing the credibility of domestic policies through international agreement. International agreement might also help to define the terms of the debate and thus limit the ability of particular interests to obtain trade protection. Even when standards are not held in common, labeling and rules of origin could permit consumers to exercise their discretion by choosing from whom they buy. Nonetheless, there are also gains to be had in allowing considerable scope for the application of different policies, particularly when effects are either borne locally or operate only through international markets. Nations that share a common labor market because of free immigration flows might find a greater interest in increased harmonization, although even here, as the U.S. experience shows, a considerable diversity in standards and practices can be sustained within a single market.

References

Allen, Steven G. 1993. "Technology and the Wage Structure." North Carolina State University.

Arthuis, Jean M. 1993. "Delocalisations—Rapport d'Information." Paris: Senate of France.

Baily, Martin Neil, and Robert J. Gordon. 1988. "The Productivity Slowdown, Measurement Issues and the Explosion of Computer Power." *Brookings Papers on Economic Activity 2*: 347–431.

Baldwin, Robert E., and Glen G. Cain. 1994. "Trade and U.S. Relative Wages: Some Preliminary Results." Summer Institute paper. Cambridge, Mass.: National Bureau of Economic Research.

Berman, Eli, John Bound, and Zvi Griliches. 1992. "Changes in the Demand for Skilled Labour within U.S. Manufacturing Industries: Evidence from the Annual Survey of Manufacturing."

Berman, Eli, Stephen Machin, and John Bound. 1994. "Implications of Skill-Biased Technological Change: International Evidence." Paper presented at the National Bureau of Economic Research, Cambridge, Mass.

Bhagwati, Jagdish N. 1971. "The Generalized Theory of Distortions and Welfare." In *Trade, Balance of Payments and Growth: Papers in International Economics in Honor of Charles P. Kindleberger*, edited by Jagdish Bhagwati and others. Rotterdam: North Holland.

———. 1991. "Free Traders and Free Immigrationists: Strangers or Friends?" Working Paper 20. New York: Russell Sage Foundation.

Binswanger, Hans. 1974. "A Microeconomic Approach to Induced Innovation." *Economic Journal* 84 (December): 940–58.

Blackburn, McKinley L., David E. Bloom, and Richard B. Freeman. 1990. "The Declining Economic Position of Less-Skilled American Men." In *A Future of Lousy Jobs?* edited by Gary Burtless, 31–76. Brookings.

Borjas, George J., Richard B. Freeman, and Lawrence F. Katz. 1992. "On the Labour Market Effects of Immigration and Trade." Discussion Paper 1556. Harvard Institute of Economic Research, Harvard University.

Borjas, George J., and Valerie A. Ramey. 1993. "Foreign Competition, Market Power and Wage Inequality: Theory and Evidence." Working Paper 4556. Cambridge, Mass.: National Bureau of Economic Research.

———. 1994. "Time-Series Evidence on the Sources of Trends in Wage Inequality." *American Economic Review* 84 (May, *Papers and Proceedings, 1993*): 10–16.

Bound, John, and George Johnson. 1992. "Changes in the Structure of Wages in the 1980s: An Evaluation of Alternative Explanations." *American Economic Review* 82 (June): 371–92.

———. 1995. "What are the Causes of Rising Wage Inequality in the United States." Federal Reserve Bank of New York, *Economic Policy Review* 1 (1): 9–17.

Boyer, Robert. 1995. "Training and Employment in the New Production Models." *OECD Science Technology Industry Review* 15: 105–32.

Brown, Drusilla K., Alan V. Deardorff, and Robert M. Stern. 1993. "International Labour Standards and Trade: A Theoretical Analysis." Discussion Paper 333. University of Michigan, Research Forum on International Economics.

Buiges, Pierre-André, and Alexis Jacquemin. 1994. "Low-Wage Countries and Trade with the European Union." Discussion Paper 9491. Institut de Recherches Economiques et Sociales, Louvain-la-Neuve, Belgium.

Bureau of Labor Statistics (BLS). 1991.

Burtless, Gary. 1995. "International Trade and the Distribution of Earnings." *Journal of Economic Literature.*

Cepii. 1994. *Le Lettre du Cepii.*

Collingsworth, Terry, J. William Goold, and Pharis Harvey. 1994. "Time for a New Global Deal." *Foreign Affairs* (January–February): 8–13.

Collins, Susan. 1985. "Technical Progress in a Three-Country Ricardian Model with a Continuum of Goods." *Journal of International Economics* 19 (August): 171–79.

Cooper, Richard N. 1993. *Environment and Research: Policies for the World Economy*. Brookings.

Cutler, David, and Lawrence Katz. 1992. "Macroeconomic Performance and the Disadvantaged." *Brookings Papers on Economic Activity 2*: 1–74.

Davis, Steven J. 1992. "Cross-Country Patterns of Change in Relative Wages." *1992 Macroeconomics Annual (NBER)*. Cambridge, Mass.

Davis, Steven J., and John Haltiwanger. 1991. "Wage Dispersion between and within U.S. Manufacturing Plants, 1963–1986." *Brookings Papers on Economic Activity: Microeconomics*: 115–80.

Deardorff, Alan V., and Paul N. Courant. 1989. "On the Likelihood of Factor Price Equalization with Non-Traded Goods." University of Michigan.

Deardorff, Alan V., and Dalia S. Hakura. 1994. "Trade and Wages— What Are the Questions?" In *Trade and Wages: Leveling Wages Down?* edited by Jagdish Bhagwati and Marvin H. Kosters, 76–107. Washington: American Enterprise Institute.

Deardorff, Alan V., and Robert Staiger. 1988. "An Interpretation of the Factor Content of Trade." *Journal of International Economics* 24 (February): 93–107.

Dickens, William T., and Kevin Lang. 1988. "Why It Matters What We Trade: A Case for Active Policy." In *The Dynamics of Trade and Employment*, edited by Laura Tyson, William T. Dickens, and John Zysman, 87–112. Cambridge: Ballinger.

Dollar, David. 1986. "Technological Innovation, Capital Mobility and the Product Cycle in North-South Trade." *American Economic Review* 76 (1): 177–90.

Ehrenberg, Ronald G. 1994. *Labor Markets and Integrating National Economies*. Brookings.

Ethier, William. 1984. "Higher Dimension Trade Theory." In *Handbook of International Economics*, edited by Ronald W. Jone. Amsterdam: North Holland.

EuroStat. 1992. *Labor Costs, 1988*, vol. 1: *Principal Results* (Luxembourg).

Fahrer, Jerome, and Andrew Pease. 1994. "International Trade and the Australian Labour Market." In *International Integration of the Aus-*

tralian Economy, edited by Phillip Lowe and Jacqueline Dwyer, 177–232. Sydney: Reserve Bank of Australia.

Feenstra, Robert, and Gordon Hanson. 1994. *Foreign Investment, Outsourcing and Relative Wages*. Columbia University Press.

Freeman, Richard. 1991. "Skill Differentials in Canada in an Era of Rising Labor Market Inequality." Working Paper 3827. Cambridge, Mass.: National Bureau of Economic Research.

———. Forthcoming. "Will Globalization Dominate U.S. Labor Market Outcomes?" In *Imports, Exports, and the American Worker*, edited by Susan Collins. Brookings.

Freeman, Richard B., and Lawrence F. Katz. 1991. "Industrial Wage and Employment Determination in an Open Economy." In *Immigration, Trade and the Labour Market*, edited by John M. Abowd and Richard Freeman, 235–59. University of Chicago Press.

———. 1994. "Rising Wage Inequality: the United States Versus Other Advanced Countries." In *Working under Different Rules*, edited by Richard Freeman. New York: Russell Sage Foundation.

Galbraith, James K., and Paulo Du Pin Calmon. 1993. "Wage Change, Trade Performance in U.S. Manufacturing Industries." Lyndon B. Johnson School of Public Affairs, University of Texas, Austin.

Gaston, Noel, and Daniel Trefler. 1992. "Union Wage Sensitivity to Trade and Protection: Theory and Evidence." Paper presented at American Economic Association meetings.

Goldsmith, James. 1993. *The Trap*. New York: Carrol & Graf.

Grossman, Gene M. 1982. "Import Competition from Developed and Developing Countries." *Review of Economics and Statistics* (May): 271–81.

———. 1984. "International Competition and the Unionized Sector." *Canadian Journal of Economics* 17 (August): 541–56.

———. 1987. "The Employment and Wage Effects of Import Competition in the United States." *Journal of International Integration* 2: 1–23.

Helpman, Elhanan, and Paul Krugman. 1985. *Market Structure and Foreign Trade*. MIT Press.

Hicks, John. 1953. "An Inaugural Lecture: The Long Run Dollar Problem." *Oxford Economic Papers* 5 (June): 117–35.

Jackson, John H., William J. Davey, and Alan O. Sykes. 1995. *Legal Problems of International Economic Relations*. St Paul, Minn.: West Publishing.

Johnson, George E., and Frank P. Stafford. 1992. "International Competition and Real Wages." Paper presented at American Economic Association meetings.

———. 1993. "International Competition and Real Wages." *American Economic Review* 83 (2): 127–30.

Juhn, Chinui, Kevin M. Murphy, and Brooks Pierce. 1993. "Wage Inequality and the Rise in the Returns to Skill." *Journal of Political Economy* 101 (3): 410–42.

Katz, Lawrence F., Gary Loveman, and David Blanchflower. 1992. *A Comparison of Changes in the Structure of Wages in Four OECD Countries*. Harvard University.

Katz, Lawrence F., and Kevin Murphy. 1992. "Changes in Relative Wages in the United States, 1963–87: Supply and Demand Factors." *Quarterly Journal of Economics* 107 (February): 35–78.

Katz, Lawrence F., and Lawrence H. Summers. 1989. "Industry Rents: Evidence and Implications." *Brookings Papers on Economic Activity: Microeconomics*: 209–91.

Kim, Dae Il, and Peter Mieszkowski. 1995. "The Effects of International Trade and Outsourcing on Relative Factor Prices." Rice University. Paper presented at University of Essex.

Krueger, Alan B. 1995. "Labor Market Shifts and the Price Puzzle Revisited." Princeton University.

Krugman, Paul, R. 1979. "A Model of Innovation, Technology Transfer and the World Distribution of Income." *Journal of Political Economy* 87 (April): 253–66.

———. 1992. "The Right, the Rich, and the Facts." *American Prospect* 11 (Fall): 19–31.

———. 1995a. *Technology, Trade and Factor Prices*. Stanford University.

———. 1995b. "Growing World Trade: Causes and Consequences." *Brookings Papers on Economic Activity 1*: 327–62.

Larre, Benedicte. 1995. "The Impact of Trade on Labour Markets: An Analysis by Industry." Working Paper Series 6. OECD Jobs Study. Paris.

Lawrence, Colin, and Robert Z. Lawrence. 1985. "Manufacturing Wage Dispersion: An End Game Interpretation." *Brookings Papers on Economic Activity 1*: 47–116.

Lawrence, Robert Z. 1990. "An Analysis of the U.S. Current Account." *Brookings Papers on Economic Activity 2*: 343–82.

Lawrence, Robert Z., Albert Bressand, and Takatoshi Ito. 1996. *A Vision for the World Economy: Openness, Diversity, and Cohesion*. Brookings.

Lawrence, Robert Z., and Carolyn Evans. 1996. "Trade and Wages: Insights from the Crystal Ball." Working Paper 5633. Cambridge, Mass.: National Bureau of Economic Research.

Lawrence, Robert Z., and Robert E. Litan. 1986. *Saving Free Trade: A Pragmatic Approach*. Brookings.

Lawrence, Robert Z., and Matthew Slaughter. 1993. "Trade and U.S. Wages in the 1980s: Giant Sucking Sound or Small Hiccup?" *Brookings Papers on Economic Activity: Microeconomics*: 161–210.

Leamer, Edward. 1991. "Effects of a U.S. Mexico Free Trade Agreement." Discussion paper. Cambridge, Mass.: National Bureau of Economic Research.

———. 1992. "Wage Effects of a U.S.-Mexican Free Trade Agreement." Working Paper 3991. Cambridge, Mass.: National Bureau of Economic Research.

———. 1994. "Trade, Wages and Revolving Door Ideas." Working Paper 4716. Cambridge, Mass.: National Bureau of Economic Research.

———. 1996. "What's the Use of Factor Contents?" Working Paper 5448. Cambridge, Mass.: National Bureau of Economic Research.

———. Forthcoming. "A Trial Economist's View of U.S. Wages and Globalization." In *Imports, Exports, and the American Worker*, edited by Susan Collins. Brookings.

Leibenstein, Harvey. 1966. "Allocative Efficiency Versus X-Efficiency." *American Economic Review* 56: 392–415.

Lynch, Lisa M. 1995. "The Growing Wage Gap: Is Training the Answer?" Federal Reserve Bank of New York, *Economic Policy Review* 1 (1): 54–60.

MacDonald, James M. 1994. "Does Import Competition Force Efficient Production?" *Review of Economics and Statistics* 76 (November): 721–27.

Machin, Stephen. 1994. "Changes in the Relative Demand for Skills in the UK Labour Market." In *Acquiring Skills: Market Failures, Their Symptoms and Policy Responses*, edited by Alison Booth and Dennis Snower. Cambridge University Press.

McKinsey. 1992. *Service Sector Productivity*. Washington: Global Institute.

MacPherson, David A., and James B. Stewart. 1990. "The Effect of International Competition on Union and Non-Union Wages." *Industrial and Labor Relations Review* 43 (4): 434–46.

Messerlin, Patrick A. 1995. *The Impact of Trade and Foreign Direct Investment on Labor Markets: The French Case.* Working Paper Series 9. OECD Jobs Study.

Mishel, Lawrence, and Jared Bernstein. 1994. Economic Policy Institute.

Murphy, Kevin, and Finis Welch. 1991. "The Role of International Trade in Wage Differentials." In *Workers and Their Wages*, edited by Marvin Kosters. Washington: American Enterprise Institute.

Neven, Damien, and Charles Wyplosz. 1994. "Trade and European Labor Markets."

Oliveira-Martins, Joaquim. 1994. "Market Structure, Trade and Industry Wages." *OECD Economic Studies* 22 (Spring): 131–54.

Oman, Charles. 1996. "The Policy Challenges of Globalisation and Regionalisation. Policy brief.

Organization for Economic Cooperation and Development (OECD). 1993. *Employment Outlook.*

———. 1994. *Jobs Study, Evidence and Explanations.*

Orr, Ann C., and James A. Orr. 1984. "Job Cuts Are Only One Means Firms Use to Counter Imports." *Monthly Labor Review* 107 (6): 39–41.

Ravenga, Ana L. 1992. "Exporting Jobs? The Impact of Import Competition on Employment and Wages in U.S. Manufacturing." *Quarterly Journal of Economics* 107 (February): 255–82.

Reich, Robert B. 1991. *The Work of Nations.* Knopf.

Rodrik, Dani. Forthcoming. *Labor Standards.* Overseas Development Council.

Rowthorn, Robert. 1994. "Unemployment, Trade and Capital Formation in the OECD." Paper prepared for UNCTAD. Cambridge University.

Rowthorn, Robert, and Sir John Wells. 1987. *Deindustrialization and Foreign Trade.* Cambridge University Press.

Sachs, Jeffrey, and Howard Shatz. 1994. "Trade and Jobs in U.S. Manufacturing." *Brookings Papers on Economic Activity 1*: 1–84.

———. Forthcoming. "International Trade and Wage Inequality in the United States: Some New Results." In *Imports, Exports, and the American Worker*, edited by Susan Collins. Brookings.

Sakurai, Norihisa. 1995. "Structural Change and Employment: Empirical Evidence for 8 OECD Countries." *Science Technology Industry Review* 15: 133–77.

Scherer, F. M. 1992. *International High-Technology Competition.* Harvard University Press.

Schwab, Klaus, and Claude Smadja. 1994. "Power and Policy: The New Economic World Worder." *Harvard Business Review* (November–December): 40–50.

Slaughter, Matthew J. 1993. "International Trade, Multinational Corporations and American Wage Divergence in the 1980s." MITIPC Working Paper 93-010WP. November.

———. 1994. "The Impact of Internationalization on U.S. Income Distribution." In *Finance and the International Economy 8: The Amex Bank Review Prize Essays*, edited by Richard O'Brien, 143–58. Oxford University Press.

Steil, B. 1994. "'Social Correctness' Is the New Protectionism." *Foreign Affairs* 73 (January–February): 14–20.

Stolper, Wolfgang, and Paul A. Samuelson. 1941. "Protection and Real Wages." *Review of Economic Studies* (November): 58–73.

UNCTC. 1991.

United Nations Conference on Trade and Development (UNCTAD). 1994. *World Investment Report*. Geneva.

United States Council of Economic Advisors. 1995. *Economic Report of the President*. Government Printing Office.

Williamson, Jeffrey. 1991. "Productivity and American Leadership: A Review Article." *Journal of Economic Literature* 29 (March): 51–68.

Wood, Adrian. 1991. "The Factor Content of North-South Trade in Manufactures Reconsidered." *Weltwirtschaftliches Archiv* 127 (4): 719–42.

———. 1994. *North-South Trade, Employment and Inequality*. Oxford: Clarendon Press.

———. 1995. "Trade, Technology and the Declining Demand for Unskilled Labour." *Journal of Economic Perspectives*.

World Bank. 1995. *Global Economic Prospects and the Developing Countries*. Washington.

Index